TESTOSTERONE, TURKEYS AND DOLLY

Observations from a Small Town Columnist
from *NOTES FROM THE COAST*

104 columns, 2012-2014

Doreen
We have a long history for not being
family + I think of you that way.
I hope this book makes you
laugh. I'm told by the people
of Tillamook County who read
my weekly column, I make them
think and laugh, that I'm a
good columnist. I'm beginning to
believe them

SCHUBERT MOORE

Schubert
(I designed it all)

Stunning Praise for Schubert Moore

"Sure, I've laughed at his columns. I've even forwarded a few, but the man is disturbed." Carolyn Germane, artist.

"He has only a rudimentary grasp of science, but if his meds have been adjusted, he can be pretty amusing." Jimmie Britton, Army Corps of Engineers

"He's hilarious. Therapy might help." John Schindelar, Teacher

"I've known him for a long time. He's funny. Just don't hurt him." Dave Canoy, Scientist.

"Most of what you've heard is not true," Dr. John Tenny, CEO eCOVE, LLC.

"We've found if you encourage him, he just writes more. Try to keep that in mind." Stephanie Tull, Florist

"Despite that incident in Portland, he puts together a pretty good column." Janet Britton, retired HR manager, Fortune 500 Company, grandmother.

"I told him if he came out with this book, I'd buy it. I hope that's not why he did it." Neil Johnson, U. S. Army, Retired.

"I want my log splitter back, dammit." Dr. Dan Matlock, Whidbey Island.

"His firewood is the best." Gary Parrett, neighbor.

Dedication

God help the friends and relatives of writers. This book is dedicated to my spouse and proofreader, Joani Moore, my friends and relatives, you know who you are, and my neighbors in Tillamook County.

I owe a special thanks to Steve Hungerford who first gave me the chance to practice on one of his newspapers while I learned how to become a columnist.

Preface

My reading audience tells me weekly I doing a good job. I'm beginning to believe them. It's a bit of a shame it took me so long to find my calling. Better late to the party, I guess, than not at all.

This book is two years of weekly columns, written for and published by the Headlight Herald, the paper of record for Tillamook County, Oregon. My plan is to publish a book, a collection of columns, every two years.

Since I don't buy stereotypes of any flavor, my neighbors are just like your neighbors. Most of them love their children, worry about their county and country, can be incredibly small-minded and mean, as your neighbors can be, as you and I can be on occasion, and at the same time, give more to others as a percentage of their net worth than Bill Gates. I'm proud to know most of them

A good portion of my neighbors work physically hard day to day. This is an agricultural county with a long coastline. There is much labor to be done. Their hands are hard as their thighs. I have seen a man in his seventies bend over a broken machine on his knees on concrete for eight hours. I have met a woman who worked a full shift cutting broccoli while raising her family of six and eighty-five foster children, twelve at a time, baking bread not by the loaf but by the dozens.

There are also people in Tillamook County of vast education and experience with stunning vision, as urbane as any New Yorker.

For you language purists, you're aware English has no third person, singular, gender-neutral pronoun. It's not my fault. I will be substituting "they" or "them" for "he or she" or "his or her," which I refuse to use.

Table of Contents

Prologue

My friend and neighbor Carol told me recently, not everyone likes your columns.

You've had complaints? I asked.

A few, she said.

Really? Give me an example?

Santa Claus, she said.

I was dumbfounded. Santa Claus?

Yes, she said, the column where you questioned the wisdom of teaching our kids about Santa Claus.

But I wasn't serious, I protested, I was trying to be funny.

They didn't laugh, she said.

You've got to be kidding. They were upset because I teased about Santa Claus? I write a humor column. I poke fun at us to help us learn more about ourselves. I don't mean those things literally.

Some of your readers don't know that. They don't 'get' you. Don't get the wrong impression, you've lot a lot of fans, but some read you literally.

At this point, I decided to write you a letter:

Dear Reader,

Most of the time I'm trying to be funny. I use satire, sarcasm, irony, absurdity, exaggeration and all the other tools of the humorist, where you don't actually mean what you say as a way to get at the truth.

The best-known example of a tongue-in-cheek humorist is Jonathan Swift. In his 1729 essay, "A Modest Proposal," he suggested the Irish, who were in a famine, eat their children. I know, gross, right? But see, he didn't mean the Irish were supposed to actually add to their diet sautéed baby. He was using satire to draw attention to the plight of the poor and the hypocrisy and heartlessness of the ruling class, slavery being our very own example.

I'm trying to write like Jonathon Swift. Actually, I'm trying to write like Joel Stein, Dave Barry, Mike Royko, Will Rogers and the gold standard of humorists, Mark Twain. One thing we all have in common, we're professional smart alecks.

We're the jesters, the jokesters, the tricksters, the clowns who open the power structure to reveal truth behind façade. Prometheus in Greek mythology, raven and coyote in Native American literature, Brer Rabbit in African American literature, Jack and the Beanstalk and Hansel and Gretel in European culture, and in more recent examples in our own culture, Charlie Chaplain, The Cat in the Hat, Bugs Bunny, and Bart Simpson. Humorists are the canaries in the mineshaft, or to mix my metaphors, we pull the tiger's tail so you don't have to. Do you really need, you might be wondering, another sarcastic, disrespectful, irreverent, class clown?

The first casualty of a dictatorship is comedy. You can trust me. I'll never make you goosestep.

An attempt was made on the life of Danish cartoonist Kurt Westergaard for his cartoons of Mohammed. He locked himself in a safe room while a whacko chopped at it with an axe. A Palestinian cartoonist took a bullet to the head. Jaime Garzon a noted satirist was killed by a motorcycle gunman. One of the greatest living writers, Salman Rushdie, has been on the run with a bounty on his head for decades. Mocking the powerful is the quickest way to get in trouble, but it's the job of the humorist to speak truth to power.

After King Lear gave his kingdom to his daughters who abandoned him, his jester told him, you're old, Uncle. You should be wise by now.

When you read me, put a grain of salt under your tongue because mine's usually in my cheek. I devote many hours a week to you, more than you would believe, certainly more than I intended when I started, to inform you, to make you chuckle, but more deviously to make you think. I'm Toto, the little dog pulling back the drapes as a man behind the curtain says, pay no attention to that man behind the curtain. I want you to pay attention.

Besides, Santa and I are tight.

Schubert Moore

Be Thankful, Dolly Parton

Thanksgiving is a holiday celebrated primarily in the U.S. Canadian Thanksgiving has the advantage of being the second Monday in October, which allows Christmas carols to be played in August. Celebration often extends to the weekend that falls closest to the holiday, or February, whichever is longer.

In the United States, the modern Thanksgiving holiday is traced to a poorly documented 1621 celebration, meaning I can say about anything I want. At Plymouth in present-day Massachusetts prompted by a good harvest, Indians gave us corn, yams, turkey and dressing, pumpkin pie and after dinner smokes and in return, we, well, you know what we did.

During the revolutionary period, the war so failed to occupy all George Washington, John Hancock, and the Continental Congress' time, they had the leisure to issue a lot of political proclamations, one of which proclaimed the first nation-wide thanksgiving celebration in America marking November 26, 1789, as a day of public thanksgiving and prayer to be observed by acknowledging God was on their side. Besides everyone knows God loves an underdog.

Thanksgiving started out as a religious holiday, but now it's about the dinner, as long as it doesn't last past half time. The centerpiece of the dinner is a poultry so bred to resemble Dolly Parton it frequently falls over and requires the children of poultry farmers to, as part of their chores, the truth, go out in the early morning and stand up the turkeys. Dolly's personal assistant has the same chore.

Each family has its own cherished traditions. My father took it as a matter of honor to buy the largest turkey in the city. My mother had him lift it into the oven where it was then cooked to perfection under her loving attention until the white meat resembled sheetrock. Fortunately, if it was a little dry, my mother made great gravy using a part of the turkey called giblets, which are impolite to discuss in mixed company.

One Thanksgiving tradition is forcing your relatives to eat a pie made from a large orange squash. I don't see why we can't use the jack o' lantern from Halloween. Waste not, want not, I say. Make sure to remove the candle wax.

We should say something about cranberries. Cranberries come in a can. Don't be fooled by so-called raw cranberries, which are, an unknown fact, a by-product of plastics research, similar to those displays of fake fruit on the dining room table of relatives who make more money than you. Cranberries pull date is much earlier than when the last of the turkey is consumed, sometime in the spring, and it is a violation of the law to possess cranberries any other time of the year, like removing pillow tags.

It is now fashionable to serve nontraditional meat on Thanksgiving. You can find organic gnu or octopus at your local Whole Foods. Octopus should be massaged for at least forty-five minutes to render it edible. Make sure to reserve the ink. Along with pumpkin, it creates that festive combination of black and orange where, another unknown fact, Oregon State University got its colors.

When my mother finally figured out she could make her daughter feel guilty enough to pick up the family tradition, I called my sister. How's the turkey coming? Okay, I guess. Did you stuff it? Stuff it? No, I didn't stuff it. It already had stuff inside.

I apologize for comparing Dolly Parton to a turkey. My wife and I love Dolly Parton, but something has happened to her face. We saw her in a movie recently and had to quit watching her, it made us so sad. We thought maybe she'd been in a car accident, but it was worse. We're afraid she thought she wasn't beautiful anymore and tried to use Joan Rivers' plastic surgeon to make her look young again, or worse, Kenny Rogers'.

Didn't Dolly have anyone to tell her, you're beautiful, and you'll always be beautiful, even when you're old and wrinkled?

You don't have to do it. You don't have to open up your skin and vacuum out your fat. You don't have to tuck your tummy, a cute phrase for major surgery. You don't have to blow up your breasts, stretch your skin, move your hairline, inject your buttocks, remove part of your neck, plump your lips, change your eyelids, or paralyze your face with poison. Women use even more extreme measures.

Being beautiful isn't what you see. It's what you do. If you have someone to tell you, be thankful. If you don't, I'll tell you. You're beautiful.

Raccoons = 3, Us = Zip

Raccoons are smarter than I am. This may not be news if you've tried to get rid of raccoons or read my columns. Raccoons are like those people, you know the ones, the really pretty people, the ones driving BMW's, whose work clothes are nicer than our good ones, and they wash their food before they eat it?

You know the people who show up at meetings with better arguments than ours and everybody likes them even if we're a little afraid of them and it would be no problem for them to climb up to our deck and eat all our birdseed?

You know the people whose kids get all the scholarships and they don't even need them while my kids have to scavenge like dogs for leftovers?

They have these perfect smiles with really big teeth and I don't know if they're smiling, or showing their teeth so I'll keep my distance. At meetings when we make our argument, they bare their big teeth and make this breathy sound that reminds me of something I saw in a nature show just before the deep-voiceover narrator says something about winnowing out the weak completes the cycle of nature.

My neighbor across the street, Mr. Green, wanted to feed birds. He put out a feeder. The raccoons ate the birdseed. Mr. Green put up a birdfeeder designed to protect birdseed. He went out the next morning with a cup of coffee. The birdseed was gone and so was the bird feeder.

Mr. Green constructed a bird feeder. Mrs. Green said Mr. Green had bobatized it. Mr. Green's first name was Bob. Bobatized means reinforced to withstand attack with the exception of a direct nuclear hit. The birdfeeder was on the ground, torn apart, and the pieces along with a little birdseed were scattered about. The message was pretty clear, since the raccoons pooped on the pieces.

Mr. Green was a vice-president of Budweiser. Mr. Green was used to getting his own way and he wasn't about to be mocked by furry creatures hiding behind masks that reminded him of lesser VP's he defeated daily in VP meetings.

I dropped by his house that night. Mr. Green was knowledgeable which meant he knew raccoons are nocturnal. Mr. Green was sitting on his deck in the dark talking to himself with three-fingers of scotch and a Glock. I didn't hear any gunfire that night although the next morning Mrs. Green said he emptied a clip. I didn't see any 911 emergency vehicles at Mrs. Parrot's house located just the other side of the ex-birdfeeder. I saw her gardening the next day. She didn't call the police but she did express an opinion about Mr. Green.

I tried to keep raccoons away from our birdseed with an electrified fence. I have to admit it was satisfying to see a raccoon come in contact with the fence. I've never seen anything move that fast. The raccoon ran off the deck and immediately held a VP meeting with four other raccoons. They decided not to seek a hostile takeover at this time. The fence worked for a while, but they eventually found a way around it. They're smarter than I am.

There was this important local issue and most of us felt one way and a few with more money felt another way and they brought in these pretty raccoon-like people with tans in Oregon and expensive graphics. They came around and shook our hands. We had to shake their small, prehensile hands or it would have revealed poor breeding.

After the meeting was over I felt the issue had been decided in our favor, but some time later I found all our birdseed was missing.

A Father Is Listening

The words, the audience is listening, appear on the screen. The THX Dolby movie sound system promo begins, faintly ominous as two halves of a musical chord rise and fall simultaneously to the limits of hearing.

If you're in any way responsible for the welfare of a subadult, you may be convinced your audience is deaf, but I will tell you, even though your child may have the zombie gaze only electronics can induce, your audience is listening.

Nothing will send alarm bells going off in your head like your son quoting your words back to you in a room full of friends and relatives. Josh said, Dad, I'll always remember what you said about scotch whiskey. I wracked my brain. What could I have possibly said about alcohol to my preteen son other than don't? They will now have proof I should have never been entrusted with raising a child. Everyone is listening.

What was that? I asked.

You said none of it tastes as good as a strawberry milkshake.

Recently I asked my son Patrick if he remembered any of my words. He reached back two decades and said, you told me on my wedding day, always have health insurance. On the phone he can't see me blush over the prosaic comment that should have been poetic on that poetic day.

I remember my sons' words more than mine. We were taken to Canada by a friend to meet her friends. Josh said, I'd like to propose a toast. My wife Joani and I betrayed alarm. Josh had never proposed a toast in his life. What toast could a six-year-old make? He raised his glass of Coke and said, to

Canada, and all her fine people. Joani and I looked at each other, dumbfounded.

Six years later, Josh said, I want to change my name. Why, I asked, his words, I was convinced, evidence of my failure as a father. Josh said, for a Christmas present. I want to add my grandfather's family name Colburn to my middle name to honor him.

In a note in a gift, Josh said, thank you for all the things you've said, but more than that, all the things you haven't.

When my first wife Wanda and I realized our marriage had been a mistake, we held each other and said goodbye. And then it came time to say goodbye to Patrick. I would be moving from Texas to Oregon. Although he was not three, he seemed to know. He looked up at me with eyes that might as well have been gun barrels. In the years since, I never told him that over the next year I often woke myself in the middle of the night, sobbing. He comes to the coast to visit every summer. I'm happy to say we're friends.

Sometimes a son's words are more than I can bear. Some years ago Patrick, now a man, and I went for a walk at night. We were trying to kill two hours before taking him to the airport. I could tell he was working himself up to say something important. As we walked along he finally brought it up, my leaving him thirty years earlier.

The audience is listening.

He gave me three words.

I took his words and mouthed them like hard candy. They melted and overcame me with their sweetness.

He said, I forgive you.

Near-Life Experience

Dr. Parnia of Stonybrook Medical Center is doing research into near-death experiences. I had a near-death experiences myself recently. I asked Nettie who runs the Sportsman Pub N Grub if she couldn't speed up her service some.

While I was out and headed toward a bright light, I remembered I had a couple questions I'd always wanted to ask if I ever got the chance. His answers:

The secret to the Universe? Oh, come on. You haven't figured that one out by now? It's so obvious. Music.

My original design was hunter-gatherer, just eat what you come across. That's one of the things wrong with you people. You take a simple idea and go crazy. So now we've got molecular gastronomy.

Farming wasn't a bad idea. That's why I gave you brains. Raise a couple cows, plant a garden. Once again, you take a simple idea and we end up with Nebraska. And don't even get me started on smart phones. And the Egyptians went way overboard with the pyramid thing. They do have a simple elegance, I have to admit. Better than the Eiffel Tower. The Greeks were a hoot. Logic. It's like statistics. You can prove anything. You can prove I don't exist. What a riot.

Big miscommunication about the resting-on-the-seventh-day thing. I don't get tired. I could have gone on indefinitely. And yours wasn't my first, you know.

Of course, it's all Middle Ages to me.

The Plague? You're fault. I kept telling you cities are a bad idea. Babel. Gomorrah. You people can't take a hint. Spread out.

The Holocaust? I had nothing to do with that. You'll have to ask Luce. He's down there. You won't be needing the sweater.

Pain? Gets you to focus.

I liked Gandhi. What a clothes horse. The robe and the glasses, the man understood fashion, elegance in simplicity.

Cathedrals, mosques, tabernacles, churches? Credit for effort, but you keep missing the point.

The Renaissance? I did most of it. You wouldn't want to know how much I helped Michelangelo. You think a mere mortal could have done David?

The Modern Age? You people crack me up. That's what you said in the Stone Age. Have to give you credit for the computer, though. You did a heck of a job with base two, just ones and zeroes. I would have used base twelve, but that's just me.

Climate change? It's you.

Marilyn Monroe? Mute proof of my existence. Elvis was a joke, but nobody got it.

Before the Big Bang? It would blow your mind.

Latest Twitter - I work in mysterious ways.

The Northern Lights? Busted. I was showing off.

Going to the moon, I have to admit, made me proud.

I try to do something nice for you and you find a way to mess things up. Fire works and you make bombs, printing press and you've got junk mail, the internet and it's porn. I try not to get depressed because it can be bad for you.

Even I can't explain the Kardashians. Or the French, come to think of it.

I can't think of one upside to the automobile. Well, maybe the Ferrari.

Biggest disappointment? Tobacco. I told Luce, even they aren't that stupid.

You have no idea how discouraging it is for someone to kill in your name.

Your best idea? Hm. Ribs. Yeah, barbecued ribs. Hard to beat that one.

Since you asked, Green Bay, although I try not to interfere.

Thanks. I try. Sunsets are therapy.

The end of the world? I'll let you know. Actually, I probably won't.

I'll say one thing, you people are always good for a laugh.

Popeye

Everyone treats the powerful with respect, but what does it say about us, the way we treat those at the edges of our economy, the way we treat slight-of-build Randy Comstock, known by almost everyone in South Tillamook County, Oregon, by a nickname he didn't ask for, for his resemblance to the cartoon hero, Popeye.

You said you go around and help people for free? Who? Harold and Darlene Fitch up by the artichoke place. He was cutting down a tree and almost got cut in half.

In half? Yeah. Tree pinned him right across here. (Randy draws a line across his stomach.) He was cutting this big ole tree and it pins him. Nobody came so he picks up this big ole chainsaw with one hand and cut himself free.

He cut the tree while it had him pinned? Yeah. He's my hero.

It did a lot of internal damage? Yeah. He was in the hospital for the longest time. I took care of their place, fed their chickens, built 'em a ramp, widened a couple of doors.

What was your childhood like? I grew up in Alaska. Family's scattered all over. They sent me back and forth from Anchorage. I was a troublemaker. If somebody was picking on somebody else, the fight was on. I've got no use for bullies. I never back down. My dad came and got me. My parents had a lot of money. My bothers and sisters mooched off them til the money was gone. My dad is ninety. Now that he needs help, where are they? I'm the one taking care of them. They tried to give me some money once, but I wouldn't take it. I always managed to survive.

What happened in your life that changed you the most? Going to prison. Cocaine. I never sold, just used. I took the blame for somebody else so she wouldn't lose her kids. I won't say who that is.

You walk back and forth to work five miles? I can't drive legally ever again. DUI. No accident, just pulled over too many times. I don't really care. I don't need to.

Have you ever had what people would call a regular life? I had a regular job. I worked at one place for 25 years doing floor covering. I was married twice, had my own house, no kids. I wouldn't want to raise them in this world anyway.

Did you ever wish your life was like other peoples'? I think everybody wishes their life was different. A lot of people are always trying to feed me food. They think I'm starving.

Spirituality? I believe there's something. I'll find out when I die.

Accomplishments? No, not really. Well, I raised my nephews. I was their daddy, their mother, I pinned their diapers. Both have good jobs and doing real well, making big bucks. One works for TriMet.

Have you helped anybody else? All the time. Darlene. Don't remember her last name. I knew her husband, One-legged Bob. He just had one leg. She lives in Woods. It was winter and she was cold. I was give a thousand dollar woodstove for work I'd done. I gave it to her.

Are you happy? Yes. I can't cry about having to walk everywhere since I did it to myself. Everybody blames somebody else for their problems. That doesn't work. My problems are my problems. I'll work for anybody. If they need the help, I'll help them. They don't have to pay. I like to help those that are struggling.

It's All We've Got

...to see the World in a grain of sand
William Blake

Since I don't understand the Endangered Species Act, I'm the perfect person to explain it to you. The ESA says it was meant to protect critically imperiled species from extinction.

Actually, it doesn't mean that at all. You've seen the poster species for the ESA, the bald eagle, big horn sheep, cougars. There were actually posters to save the bald eagle. They worked, too. It's no longer endangered.

What the ESA means is they're trying to save fuzzy species with faces that make you go, awww. If not those, then species you can hold in your hand, like butterflies or fish. If not those then plants, like Small's milkpea. If not those, then species you can at least *see?*

If you went down to the beach and scooped up a handful of wet sand, you'd be holding about 10,000 critters called meiofauna that live in the moisture between grains of sand. You would find, as Discover Magazine tells us, a microscopic jungle of minuscule invertebrates spending their lives slithering between the sand grains by whirling hair like propellers on their heads or holding tight to the sand grains with tiny claws, as if clinging desperately to giant beach balls. And don't get me started on bacteria.

Those 22 phyla of organisms do something much more important for us than bald eagles do. They clean the sand as if it has been newly washed and without which the beach would be a decaying, stinking slick.

It's the 70's, just after the ESA came into existence, late in the evening after too much wine, after we'd been arguing this issue long past the time everyone should have gone home, and since we're men, after our voices had gotten too loud. Dave is trying to defend the ESA and I'm not having much trouble picking it apart, the holes in logic you could fly a whooping crane through. Dave is the most competitive man I know. He's not used to losing and it shows.

I love this man, this gifted scientist, this brilliant teacher who has spent the past four decades revealing to me the wonders of science with infinite patience despite my degree in English.

Memory is a funny thing. I don't remember all we said that night, but I remember how our thinking has evolved. His argument that night should have been, for all those who think it's important to still have salmon and eagles and condors, it's also important to have the Texas blind salamander and the Callippe silverspot butterfly and the Virginia sneezeweed.

You can't do it, he would say now. You can't say one species is more important than another. If you save one, you save them all. If you don't save Small's milkpea, you don't save the bald eagle.

But I do remember how he won that night. Yes, he said, the ESA is badly flawed. And then he claimed victory by using the same type of argument that saved Yosemite.

You *have* to support the Endangered Species Act, because, he said, bearing down with an unsmiling concentration I swear created heat, it's all we've got.

What the ESA doesn't tell you is that of the 1.7 million species on our planet, 90% of them don't have names and according to the Sierra Club, one of them becomes extinct every fifteen minutes.

My question is, if one of those organisms, the epsilonematid nematode, for instance, was endangered, would it get a poster?

Andy Rooney Is Dead

Andy Rooney died. His voice is my head. If you ever heard him speak, I'll bet you can hear him, too. If I use his style, maybe it would sound something like this:

There's been a lot of dying going around lately. Have you thought about dying? I'll bet you have.

I was supposed to be dead now. At least that's what I thought when I was 30 – 50 was old, 60, very old, 70, dead. Three score and ten, The Bible says. I have a 70th birthday coming up this month. How about you?

There's been a lot of births going around, too. I'm told the 7 billionth person was born recently. My wife Joani and I have our first granddaughter due this month. She'll be special, not like the other billions.

I see from the longevity tables, a girl born this month will live to 80, 75 if it's a boy.

If I make it to 70, it increases my odds. Instead of croaking at 75, I'm supposed to hit 83, 86 for Joani. Croak is a funny word. It sounds like the last gasp. Well, I guess it isn't very funny after all.

If you're a man reading this at 30, you have 47 more years, 51, ladies. Sorry, guys. The reason why is another column.

According to the tables, I have to die in the next 13 years. I wonder how it will happen?

I have a 50% chance of dying of heart attack or cancer. Heart attacks are in the lead. The chance of dying because of an accident, like being run over by a dory boat, is 4%.

I'm in pretty good shape, considering heavy drinking for 30 years. I stopped 2 years ago. I played with tobacco, spent 6 months as an exterminator breathing chlordane and diazinon, and was treated as a child for a skin condition using a newly discovered technology, x-rays. Who knew? It's a wonder I'm still here. So what's happened to you to subtract a few years from your life? I've put my faith in whole grains. Silly. What's your strategy?

It's a Sunday afternoon, a day for reflection. The Sunday afternoons used to stretch out, one after another, like two mirrors face to face, until they darkened into infinity. But it seems I can actually count them now, the Sunday afternoons, reflecting into the mirrors, one after another. I think I might be able to see the very last one.

I'd like to wish you a long life, but I want one, too, and these are averages.

July 4th Means Happy Birthday, America

Once again it's time for Mr. News Guy to explain to you the mysteries of language. Only America has July 4th and with the exception of explosives, nothing is more associated with July 4th than politicians making speeches. We here at the NOTES research department have put together this handy pocket guide in an effort to help you decipher the real meaning behind political rhetoric.

I'm not a politician, means I'd like to be, but either a) I can't get elected or b) I don't understand how government works.

I bring vital leadership, means I'm way hotter than my opponents. OMG! Have you seen them?

We need to set priorities, means I have no idea what we should be doing.

I can't advise you on this issue, means my staff is still arguing about what I should think.

That's a really good question, means my staff didn't prepare me for this question.

Times are tough right now, means there is no chance you'll get any help.

We need to get back to the basics, means I'm going to cut what you want out of the budget.

My number one priority, means my number one priority for this audience.

I've been going around the district talking to people, means I can't afford pollsters.

I know how to listen, means I can afford pollsters.

We need to take a closer look at this issue, means I've hired a pollster.

I'm not afraid to stand up for what's right, means if it polls well.

This issue is critical, means until something else polls sexier.

This is a very important issue, means you'll never pin me down.

I'm open to considering this issue, means would you like to make a contribution to my campaign fund?

We need to learn more, means delay.

It's never easy to vote to raise taxes, means it's easy to vote to raise taxes if I can find cover.

Finding cover, means blaming someone else.

Local control, means I put my secretary on it.

We need to consider that carefully, means there's no chance I'll consider it.

We need to keep in mind, means I promised something different to the last audience.

I'm a very strong supporter of this issue, means my big money is a strong support of this issue.

This is an interesting question, means I have no interest in this question.

This is a pretty frustrating issue, means I'm having trouble remembering what I said before.

We need to change the way we govern, means boy, you hated what I tried the last time.

I have a vision, means my big money has a vision.

I'm fiscally conservative, means I won't spend any of your money on projects unless they'll help me get reelected

I have a wealth of experience, means I'm a living argument for term limits.

Several aspects should have been vetted, means I'm in deep doo.

I want to spend more time with my family, means my affair is about to go public.

It was an honor to represent you, means it was an honor to represent you.

County Commissioners Endanger Species

Due to your poor performance on the quiz, it's obvious you need another stern lecture on the Endangered Species Act.

Although the numbers of marbled murrelet are shrinking world wide, I found after exhaustive research scanning Wikipedia, the responsibility for saving them rests squarely with the Tillamook County Commissioners.

Governor Kitzhaber did a bang-up job putting stable funding under our schools during his first term by instituting statewide bake sales. He's been invited back for round two to help by stopping timber sales near the marbled murrelet. This prevents us from squandering the money on roads, schools and other luxuries.

So why is the marbled murrelet endangered? It's not on the menu in any restaurant I know of, unlike the spotted owl in Jefferson County. Women don't wear hats anymore. The ESA made it illegal to trade in endangered species like whales and pygmy rabbits (12,345 pygmy rabbits equal one whale).

We'll, for one reason, they're standoffish, like those relatives of yours who have more money and drop in for a short visit on their way to someone more interesting. They want to be left alone and they don't like loud noises, which pretty much disqualifies your family. Gov. Kitzhaber accommodates the marbled murrelet by preventing Tillamook loggers from using engines when cutting trees. Handsaws are permitted.

I personally think the marbled murrelet shouldn't be coddled. The bald eagle didn't have any trouble bouncing back and we were spraying them with DDT. Eww, I can hear the marbled murrelet say. That noise is like so annoying, I won't reproduce. Puh-leeze.

Well, we need to ask ourselves, what could we do to save the marbled murrelet? One, reduce the number of Tillamook County Commissioners. With three of them it's almost impossible to know who's responsible. We need to delete Commissioners Josi and Labhart and convince Commissioner Hurliman to serve another term. He knows more loggers. Then if the marbled murrelet didn't rebound, we'd know who to blame.

Two, we waste too much money on the homeless when we could be saving endangered species. Besides, the homeless aren't endangered. That's why we decided to save the residents of Tillamook State Forest rather than the residents sleeping behind stores.

Three, since we have too many people and they crowd the marbled murrelet, we could institute a one-child policy like China has. I'm sure some days this makes good sense. You've come home exhausted after work wanting to put your feet up, have a drink and find out what's happening with the Kardashians. Instead, your family is yelling at each other.

I'm sure on at least one occasion, you've surveyed the clutter of toys and video games amidst the screaming and thought to yourself, wouldn't the marbled murrelet be a lot better off if I had fewer kids?

Then you tune out the chaos and wonder what the marbled murrelet is thinking right this very minute. You wonder if it would mind if you sat down and leaned against the Douglas Fir it's nesting in. You could finish your drink. The wind would blow real gentle like. The branches would rustle.

You promise. You wouldn't make a sound.

The Coliseum and Cold Showers

I see the Coliseum is for sale. Not the Roman one. The movie theater in Tillamook, Oregon. I can almost hear the gasps. Remember? Some of you are still here, some scattered like the wind around the globe. For all of you, a quicker beat of memory's heart when you went with your sweetie and exchanged touches in the Coliseum's darkness. At the mention of the Coliseum, some of you will need a cold shower.

When I was not more than six, I was allowed to go to the neighborhood Crest Movie Theater in Dallas, Texas, alone. I know, times were different. We had very little money, but I was given enough to buy a ticket and a candy bar.

I didn't have any understanding of what was going on at the movies. I didn't know about projectors or sound systems or how anything worked, I thought the cowboys and horses were actually there on the stage behind a magic screen. Even though later it was explained to me, I just prefer believing it's a magic screen.

About nine years ago we watched movies on a 21-inch television cube. When it became too dim to be called entertainment, Joani and I went shopping for a replacement. Flat screen monitors were now available, as was sticker shock.

At the same time we became aware of home movie theaters at a fraction of the cost of plasma. Also we had a big, blank wall. We installed a projector, a surround sound system and found to our delight we had our own movie theater. Each night we pull the curtains, dim the lights and sometimes with popcorn, the magic happens all over again in Moores' Majestic Theater.

As a child, I often smiled at my parent's displays of affection. Maybe it had to do with Dad going off to war and being unsure if he would come back. My father couldn't go to the store for eggs and milk without fully embracing my mother and a pretty serious kiss.

My father was a strict man. I never intentionally disobeyed him, with one exception. When he and my mother sent me to the Crest Theater at noon on Saturdays, I was told to come home after the short, the cartoon, the previews of coming attractions, and the double feature.

As much as I wanted to obey, I couldn't do it. I could not make myself get out of my seat and go home like I had been told to do. I was transfixed, mindlessly hypnotized by 24 frames per second of flickering light that put on the magic screen gun fights, car chases, airplanes spiraling out of control, dancing clowns and monsters rising out of primordial slime.

My father would come to get me. It would be dark by then. He would walk me home as he told me since I disobeyed and hadn't come home when I should have, I would not be allowed to go to the movies again.

To my surprise, the next Saturday, I was pushed out the door with money in my hand and told to go to the movies.

It was a long time before I figured out why. Although he had never seen a movie there, at the mention of the Crest Theater I'm guessing my father needed a cold shower.

The Virtual Library

Unlike most of my columns, some of this is the truth.

The day will come when staring at an electronic reader in a doctor's office will not prompt a total stranger patient from stopping and giving me an unasked for monologue on why he prefers actual books. He went on about the feel of it, how unnatural it was to read off a screen, as if holding four hundred sheets of beaten tree pulp was the most natural thing in the world. Then without asking my opinion, he walked off. That happens a lot.

What's unnatural? You've been staring at an illuminated screen your entire life. If you haven't, you're over seventy. You've scooped Cheerios into your mouth while watching words flicker since Burt and Ernie told you today was brought to you by the letter K.

My lovely and intelligent wife Joani reads a lot and so for our anniversary I bought her a digital reader. I downloaded a Nora Roberts novel, one of her favorite authors, from the internet. It took two minutes.

"Oh," she said, "it's one of those...," Not knowing how to finish said she'd preferred a dust buster.

Most of what's on her reader has been put there by visiting short people without permission who've changed the background and rearranged stuff. On occasion I've seen them do this with their fingers while the rest of them was asleep.

Joani has continued to read without the aid of electronics. I decide to try the electronic reading experience by downloading one of the many books my library told me were available.

I signed up for a mystery "Stick" by Elmore Leonard. I was told we had several copies. They were all checked out. I contemplated where our library kept virtual books but decided that path led to insanity.

I put a hold on it and was told it would be available in about three months. Since I had put the hold on Joani's account, I didn't receive an email telling me I had three days to download it. When I checked, I was told I missed my deadline for downloading and the wait for the next copy was three months.

I was finally successful "checking out" a virtual book, after assistance from the library. You have to wait for the librarian who knows how. You have to download library software so the digital reader could read the file. The reader must have missed Burt and Ernie.

I was enjoying the experience. I didn't lose my place when I dropped the reader. I could read in low light. I could read either black letters or white letters. It was very cool, and although unsure of its purpose. I switched back and forth several times because I could.

I probably should have paid more attention to the due date. I was approaching the second plot point where everything is at stake and all seems lost when I turned the virtual page with a flick of my finger on the screen and the book disappeared.

The digital reader was still there and the title "Stick" was still at the top of the page. It was the words. They were gone.

The Big Virtual Librarian with a pencil stuck in her virtual hair bun said, Sir, your time is up. I'll be taking your book now. No, Sir, you are not allowed to keep reading it and pay a fine. You're done, but if you'd like to get on the list for this book, the wait is three months.

Let's Hear It for Nonpartisan!

I just experienced my first nonpartisan election in Tillamook County. Actually, it's not my first. It's the first time I paid any attention. It was remarkable. There were a hundred candidates. Actually I'm exaggerating somewhat. There were seven. It just seemed like a hundred. My boss' boss' boss helped out some by endorsing one of them. (I have to be careful here. I don't want to lose my position paying me the big bucks.)

Anyway, I really didn't have to actually pay attention to what they were saying, this time, either. The instructions for the election didn't ask me to pick the most qualified, the most experience, or the most educated. It didn't ask me to vote for the one who had given the most to the community, who had the best church attendance, who was the unhappiest with the way things were being run, or who was the prettiest, male or female. If you had paid your fees and were pretty much vertical, you qualified.

We the electorate were asked to pick the two candidates who had the most votes, and I'm pretty sure we did that.

This was different than most elections I paid attention to. Previously, after thorough research and evaluation, I marked the candidates my lovely and intelligent wife Joani told me to mark.

I have a friend Jim who spends way too much time arguing with me via email. He doesn't tell me who to vote for. Good thing, because Joani wouldn't permit it. He tells me mainly to vote for no one currently holding office. He tells me he is a member of neither major party, which leaves open the Greens and Socialists, I suppose. He says he's an Independent.

I keep telling him when he votes, he's no longer an independent.

I would like to propose all elections be nonpartisan, no parties, just names of people. If you were way more interested than I and wanted your vote to actually mean something, you'd have to find out who the candidates are and if they take a good picture. Hair helps for men, smiles for women. Smiling male candidates makes the voter queasy.

It doesn't really matter what their beliefs are. They'll give up most of them half way through their first term in order to get anything done. Ask any elected official. They're more candid if you get them drunk.

Anyway, I think if we went to nonpartisan elections, it would be better all around. For one thing, it creates a smaller target for the incoming rounds of cash lobbed mortar-style into the elections by Superpacs created by the Supreme Court. It would keep foreign corruption out, meaning east of the Idaho border. Besides, if we want corruption, most of us prefer it be local.

Don't let it get out, but I was an advisor for one of the candidates. That made me a political operative, kind of like Karl Rove Lite. To prepare for my role, I watched reruns of The West Wing, the TV show about White House insiders. I tried to identify myself with one of the characters. I'm pretty sure I'm not Josh. He's too smart. I look more like Toby, if Toby was fifty years older. I just hope I wasn't the one who accidentally slept with a hooker. Joani wouldn't let me vote at all.

The Mancation

Dear Wife,

I'm writing to you from my mancation, a vacation for men, a word coined by one of the other wives, and she meant, if not ridicule, then at least amused tolerance. Nine of us have gathered for a few days to do exactly what we want. Most age groups are represented, from thirty-somethings to retired. We gathered to be men together, not much differently than the way you gather together to be women.

One of us served in the hot, wet war of Vietnam as an officer where no one wore underwear because it rotted off. He was supposed to be relieved after six months but was kept for a year until he contracted malaria.

One is now a clean-cut construction worker who learned his craft in a commune wearing shoulder-length hair and looking for enlightenment snacking on peyote.

One is a metal worker hanging on the side of tall buildings in Salem. One makes sure your water is safe, one is an atheist in a Jesuit university, one makes sure predoctors know the difference between the spleen and the pancreas, one is completing his one-hundredth triathlon in ten years, one carries a gun on his job, one writes a column.

It is not what you might be thinking, a bacchanal of empty beer bottles like a disorganized army of toy soldiers in retreat, food left out to spoil, stacks of greasy pizza boxes, visits to strip joints.

Yes, we do manly things. We river raft, make long, steep hikes to the top of things which reminds us of our mortality, but we also gather pretty rocks, visit museums, read, cook, and look up at the stars, wondering about the meaning of it all.

We do a lot that might surprise you. Nobody at the mancation has to be told to clean up after themselves. We exchange recipes. We exchange medical information. We take out the trash. We behave.

But more than anything, we talk. Occasionally we talk of victorious sports moments, fast cars and fast women we have known.

But if you overheard us you would smile in gentle surprise that our conversations sound a lot like yours. Some talk is of family, the successes or failures of our children or grandchildren. We talk about those who served our country. We worry about our conflicts overseas, about the next generation and contemplate the direction our country is headed.

We are not the fierce beasts conjured by the image of caveman. We are still bigger and stronger than you, and there are times when we abuse that advantage. Shame on us when we do. For the most part, though, we have muzzled our fangs. We sheathed our claws. We have been domesticated and we helped you do it.

We don't talk about wives, but it's not for the reasons you might suppose. Although we may have intended to run away from you for a while, to taste again the bracing salt of freedom, you can't make a meal of salt.

We hold back sharing you. We will not put you out with the rest of what's on our mind to be inspected and judged. If we didn't before, we understand now, you're too important for that.

Although it's a cliché, the words are still true, freedom is just another word for nothing left to lose. Every one of us sharing our last breakfast here has known loss and so at the end of our mancation, if we spoke of what we felt, and because we're men we wouldn't do that, we would say we're beginning to feel lonely. We all have someone we miss. It's time to go home.

Your Husband

I Interviewed Miss Oregon!!!

I'm seventy years old. I found Miss Oregon, Nichole Mead, 22, holding court at the Turnaround in Seaside. She was wearing a formal gown, heels, and holding a bouquet of roses among the tourists in tank tops and flip-flops.

Nichole Mead represents Oregon in the Miss America Pageant in Las Vegas, Nevada, on January 12, 2013. Mead is a graduate of the University of Oregon with a Bachelor of Science in Psychology and a minor in Communications.

She grew up watching the Miss Lincoln County Pageant with her mother. Becoming Miss Oregon and competing at the Miss America Pageant, the fulfillment of a lifetime dream. As Miss Oregon Mead will receive a $10,000 cash scholarship.

I was in Seaside because my son and his family had arrived on their annual visit here, and we thought a trip to the boardwalk with all the tourist kitsch would be fun. We started spinning on the Merry-go-round where I was told over the loud speaker, Sir, please do not stand up on the horses when they were moving and, Sir! Please, Sir, would you quit leaning out trying to touch people!

I asked Miss Oregon a few questions.

Schu: Where are you from?

Nicole: I'm from Newport, Oregon!

(I wonder if all beauty pageant winners speak with exclamation points.)

Schu: Have you ever been to Tillamook?

Nicole: I have! In high school! We went there a few times!

Schu: Will you be visiting us as Miss Oregon any time during the next year?

Nicole: We'll see! I hope so! My job is the official hostess of Oregon, so I'll be traveling all up and down Oregon, so definitely!

Schu: Will you be competing in Miss America?

Nicole: January 2013 for Miss America!

Schu: Is that hard? Is there a lot of training?

Nicole: There is a lot of training but then there was a lot of training for Miss Oregon!

Schu: You know, Nicole, I write a humor column. Could you say something funny?

Nicole: Goodness! I can't think of anything funny off the top of my head!

Schu: Do you mind if I have my picture taken with you?

Nicole: Not at all!

She put her left arm around me.

Did I mention to her, I wondered, that my name is Schubert Moore? I thought to myself, she may be stunningly beautiful and she may have put her left arm around me, but I can still remember my name.

After the interview I took my family to ride the bumper cars where I was admonished over the loud speaker, Sir, Sir! No head-on collisions, please!

Mr. News Guy Explains Testosterone

It's time once again for Mr. News Guy to explain to you the puzzling behavior of people in the news.

For instance, seven Oregon legislators happen to run into each other in Palm Springs, California. What were the odds? They went into a Gentlemen's Club to watch a TV basketball game but topless young women kept obscuring their view. A Gentlemen's club is a service organization dedicated to gentlemen who might be contemplating changing professions from politics to plastic surgery or gynecology.

Anyway, not one of those public servants intended to watch other men's daughters practicing what they assumed were first responders' exercises, like sliding down a pole. They were forced to. Their bodies had been taken over by the most toxic substance known to humankind - testosterone.

Testosterone compels men to become hairy and attack other men and countries. Every war from the Crusades to the Superbowl has been awash in testosterone, which cause in men uncontrolled strutting and eye rolls in women.

If you're of the male persuasion and you're wondering if you might be suffering from testosterone poisoning, here are a few telltale signs:

You bought an endloader and you're not in construction.

You were last injured just after you said, hey guys, watch this.

You use your demolition derby car to create a parking space.

You have a demolition derby car.

You measure trips in miles per beer.

You can recognize any woman you've ever met without seeing her face.

What can I do, Mr. News Guy, you might be asking, if I find I'm the victim of testosterone poisoning?

Not much. Avoid what women suggest, scented candles, sheets with a high thread-count, and a Saturday spent at Bed, Bath, and Beyond. This causes men to imagine women without clothing, but then, so do tax forms.

High on a list of women's solutions, but the worst suggestion of all, is talking about your feelings. This short-circuits what passes for high-level thought in men and often induces coma.

An alarming development in the war on testosterone poisoning is injectable testosterone available, not in back alleys, but at your doctor's office! That's what happens when we deify doctors. First they're our trusted family advisor, the next thing you know they're pushing dangerous drugs.

The average testosterone level for an (oxymoron alert!) adult male is over 400. Nature wisely turns down the volume on your testosterone level as you age so your apathetic silence will be mistaken for wisdom.

Now it is possible to score a fix of injectable testosterone at any doctor's office and maintain the same testosterone level as a young man. That's exactly what this country needs, a bunch of randy old men commanding the armed forces and invading any country with oil reserves.

Now that I think of it, that explains a lot.

Political Dictionary – Page 2

Join us for second edition of what politicians really mean when they say:

Healthcare Reform: Republicans – We're going to reform Healthcare by keeping it the same. Democrats – If we can force you to buy insurance, we can force you to wear an Obama T-shirt.

Private sector: Repubs – The source of our strength, and also when we're running a little short. Dems – Visited a couple times. Wouldn't want to live there.

Congress: Dems – Like the ex-girlfriend who kicked you out, but you're still in love. Repubs – Like the ex-wife you want to forget but you got these kids that look like you.

Taking some time away: Repubs – I don't fish. I have people do that for me. Dems – Going to the hood and pretending to be black.

Free trade: Repubs – For free trade as long as jobs going overseas are blamed on Democrats by reporters in articles. Dems – For free trade since no one reads those articles.

I like dogs: Dems – Fly the First Dog on private jet at big taxpayer expense. Repubs – Drive the First Dog at no expense and it gets plenty of fresh air.

It will take more than one term: Dems – It will take two terms to repair the legacy. Repubs – We know. We had two terms last time and still couldn't do it.

Make the world a safer place: Repubs – attack Iran. Dems – Attack Republicans.

We need a leader that will lead: Dems – Smart enough to go off script. Repubs – Smart enough to stay on script.

Efficient: Dems – Electing a Democrat in Boston. Repubs – Raising a lot of money.

Effective: Dems – Electing a Democrat in Houston. Repubs – Finding someone to spend it on.

The Constitution: Repubs – Like the Old Testament and the Ten Commandments. Dems – Like the New Testament and asking forgiveness.

Homeland Security: Repubs – It's fun to strip search Grandma. Dems – Predator drone attacks on terrorists and Republican campaign events.

Conservative Democratic: Dems – Voter with identity crisis. Repubs – Easy mark.

Conservative Republican: Repubs – Well, duh. Dems – Redundant.

Liberal Democratic: Dems – Democrat under 25. Repubs: Satan.

Liberal Republican: Repubs – Satan's helpers. Dems – an apocryphal beast like the unicorn.

Medicare: Repubs – Coverage for Republicans who lost a lot in the last downturn. Dems – Coverage for Democrats not in government.

Medicaid: Dems – Coverage for Democrats who lost a lot in the last down turn. Repubs – isn't that the new Band-Aid with Neosporin?

The direction of this country: Repubs – Is terrible. Obama hasn't been impeached yet. Dems – Is good. Obama hasn't been impeached yet.

It's the economy, Stupid: Repubs – I heard we're in a downturn. Dems – Didn't know you were watching that closely.

Immigration: Dems – Without immigration we can't get elected. Repubs – Without immigration, who'll drive our taxis?

Founding Fathers: Repubs – Their inspired words are the basis for the liberties we enjoy today. Dems – I would have lifted a grog with Franklin, but Washington looks like he needs a laxative.

Stimulate the economy: Dems – A phrase we invented to spend more money because we haven't had an original idea since FDR. Repubs – A phrase we invented to avoid paying taxes.

Energize the base: Repubs – Ivy League politician not in Congress. Dems – Chicago politician not in jail.

The American Dream: Dems – America without Republicans always compromising our efforts to lift the poor into the middle class. Repubs – America without Democrats.

The Church of the Salmonites

I'd like to tell you a story.

The Church of the Salmonites was formed in the 1980's on a sunny Saturday afternoon. The first congregation lay littered about Larry and Ielean Rouse's beach cabin in Pacific City, exhausted after fishing all day. There was Anne Price, now a loan officer for Oregon Coast Bank, her then husband John Abele, the Rouses, Canoys, Tennys, Carottas, Marcoes, and Moores. We all were either owners or renters in South Tillamook County. Without much discussion, we elected Larry Rouse Reverend of the Church. We had in common our love of salmon fishing, high-stress professional careers and a taste for beer.

It was an outdoor crash course for me. The Church knew the regs and never cheated, could identify any bird they saw at a glance, fin-clipped salmon smolts, volunteered for the SOLV beach cleanup, were whale watch volunteers. In short, they taught me to be a steward of our place.

We confused the Pacific City Winkleman Library Board when we donated $150, the proceeds of the 1st Annual Church of the Salmonites Library Fund Crap Game. They finally took the money.

We had our rituals. When Marcoes and we bought boats at the same time, Reverend Larry gathered us together for the christening, read from the Navy manual, usually something at random, in our case the proper disposal of marine bilge. He solemnly petitioned Neptune to bring fair winds and calm seas. He also prayed we all would return safe to shore. Over the years, his prayer was answered. Even though we thought our tongues were planted firmly in our cheeks, there were locked throats at those rituals, surprising us with their power.

The Church took its boats down the minefield of sandbars that make up the lower Nestucca River to fish the mouth where the river meets the Pacific Ocean. We were good. Limits were common, thirty-pound Chinook numerous, fifty-pounders on occasion.

After fishing we gathered on the edge of the tiny Nestucca bay I called The Holy Land. Over a fire we would cook sausages and boil crab and weave a net of connectedness by recounting what happened that day in stories, endlessly repeated over the years. I sometimes think the purpose of doing anything is to make a story.

Several of us have handcrafted pottery plaques fired by Carolyn Canoy declaring our existence. The Church of the Salmonites owns a brick at Kiwanda Community Center. We grew close. This place became a part of us.

What were we doing?

We were creating family, the same way Lions, Scouts, fraternities and sororities create family by bonding with ritual-blessed stories. We were trying to hold on to each other.

It didn't work. The Church of the Salmonites died. Age killed it and the occasional personal conflict. Who can say why a thing like that is no more? Groups are fragile, hard to hold. Everything has a life span. But while it lasted, ah, there was a glory there.

Want to keep someone? Tell them a story.

Why Politicians Disappoint Us

As I write this, the two major political parties just completed their national conventions. We heard the candidates say how much they love their mothers, fathers, children, wives, husbands, grandmothers and grandfathers, and a few other relatives and friends.

We were told we deserve better. We were told that gas prices are too high, house values too low, and our national character just right. Both parties told us how great we are, we the American people. We we're told we work hard, that we worry about expenses over our kitchen table, a good education for our kids, our mortgage, our jobs, and our retirement, We're told we're optimistic. We were told we never give up and these qualities were uniquely American.

That must mean members of other countries don't care about their kids, don't worry about anything, are pessimistic, and give up the first chance they get.

We were told the future relies on our kids. I don't know about you, but that isn't entirely comforting.

And then came the promises. We heard them tell us they would get jobs for everyone who doesn't have one (I don't want one). Both want to get our country going again, to start building roads, bridges, highways, houses, cars, and both major and minor appliances. Both want to pay down our debt. That's good. My father said being in debt is bad.

Both parties claim they don't like war despite the fact we're either in or just out of one, and yet we're always threatening to get into another one. Both are thankful for those who've served, died or been wounded. Both want to support our troops. No one said exactly what that means. To judge from the past, it has a lot to do with putting ribbons on things.

We were told that their programs are good, and the other party's programs are bad. We were told we have a choice and that means we're not to vote for the other party.

What are we to make of these simplistic claims? Mario Cuomo said, we run for office in poetry and we govern in prose. Prose is specific. Poetry is abstract. That means whatever we want it to mean and politicians know this.

It is the implied agreement, the way we want to be spoken to so we can fill in the details ourselves. Long before Ross Perot said, the devil is in the details, it was. When Hitler said, let's make Germany stronger, did he mean let's have the trains run on time or kill all the people we don't like?

Politicians can't tell you specifically what they'll do because they often don't know. They mean maybe they can find a way to fix the pothole in front of your house, and you mean you'll have some money left before the next paycheck, that no one will break into your car, that your kids will clean up their rooms.

Politicians run for office and speak to us in abstracts. It's what we want. If they didn't, we wouldn't vote for them. When they say, I'll make this county better, you voted for them. If they had said, to fix your roads, I'll raise your taxes, you wouldn't have. Yet we know somebody will have to pay the bill. Who do we think that would be?

We want to fill in the details. That's why the devil is in them. That's why we'll always be disappointed.

Cheap Fun

My lovely and intelligent wife Joani and I were stopped at an intersection when, turning in front of us, was a RV just like my uncle's. It was totally self-contained, with everything a starter house has, except in addition it had two freezers and a generator big enough to light Bay City in the winter.

The thing was, as it swung into the lane, we saw attached, a trailer the size of our bedroom. We burst into laughter.

If you've seen extended-cab pickups towing enough recreational equipment to furnish the Costco summer display, you might conclude it is impossible to have fun unless you spend enough to equal Lithuania's national debt.

In the interest of fair disclosure, I have to admit to one time owning a large piece of recreational equipment, one of the dory boats of Pacific City. I remember telling Joani as a justification for buying the boat, just think how much money we'd save by going into the ocean and catching all that free seafood. My wife is detail-oriented and she estimated when all the boat expenses we're figured in, we had reduced what we paid for seafood to just $42 per pound.

You've forgotten, but any toddler knows. The box is more fun than the toy. You can have more fun with your kids without selling one of them by making big bubbles for a few bucks. You'll need 20 oz Dawn dish soap, ½ c glycerin, ½ teaspoon J-Lube (used by veterinarians, available on the internet), 4.5 oz. tube K-Y Jell (ask your wife), and 1 ½ gal. water. Except for Dawn, all this stuff is much cheaper on the internet.

For each "kid", that will probably include you, too, you'll need two sticks (I use wood dowels) and a loop made of three strands braided cloth, yarn, thick cotton twine or anything that will absorb and hold the solution. Affix the loop to the end of the sticks about 1/3 of the loop apart. The bigger the loop, the bigger the bubble.

Dip the loop in the solution until it's soaked. Keep the sticks together, lift high overhead and slowly move the sticks apart. Works best in a gentle breeze. When the bubble is as big as you want, move the stick tips back together and it will pinch off the bubble. Or you can keep the sticks apart and go for length. Our record is 80 ft.

At this point, magic happens.

I have done this on the beach at Pacific City on a weekday at noon and within ten minutes there were fifty people gathered around, oohing and ahhing. I've seen adults break into uncontrolled giggles. My neighbor took the sticks away from his grandson and told him to go play.

Although I don't have a photo to document, I've made a bubble the size of a small RV.

Road Levies A Big Problem

Ex TBCC President Jon Carnahan will manage another run at a road repair levy. "There's a lot of things I need to know before I start visiting with people," Jon said.

What? What do you need to know, Jon? I beg you for the sake of our roads, don't put another road levy on the ballot.

Growing up a long time ago in a land far away, my next-door neighbor was a woman called Floy. I came into her house with her boy Bill and a hard crush on her girl Anne and sometimes ate dinner with them, two cans of something and fried meat. Everybody in the neighborhood knew everybody's business.

Floy was a loud-lunged yeller at neighbors. I never saw her in anything but a bathrobe, hair rollers, and a cigarette dangling.

Though just a boy, I wondered too what a neighbor yelled at her, "Hey, Floy, you flat-footed floozy, where is your man?"

"Wouldn't spit on her if she was on fire," she told me and winked, but I could see it hurt her.

"Why don't I have a man?" she asked her coffee cup. "It's cause I got half-grown kids."

I took a logic class once. One thing we studied was logical fallacies. My favorite logical fallacy is post hoc ergo propter hoc, meaning just because one thing follows another doesn't mean it's caused by it.

Some years ago, I was in the checkout line of the Pacific City Market. There was a woman ahead of me discussing an upcoming levy to construct a new high school. The woman was trying to explain to the checker, they're telling me we have to have a new high school because the old building is falling down. They say it isn't safe. The woman was thoughtful for a bit and then said, that can't be true. Why not? the checker asked, scanning the woman's Cool Whip and Twinkies. The woman moved her fingertip from her chin and shook it at the checker. Because my kids are going to school there.

According to the Library Director, a Tillamook man had taken his daughter regularly to Story Time at the library since she was in diapers. He had been petitioned to vote in favor of the new library levy, but I don't support it, he said. If it doesn't pass, I won't waste any more time on politics. I'll just take my daughter to Story Time at the library.

When the hillsides above clear cuts slide into streams and block roads, the experts hired by the timber companies testify the slides are inevitable due to the steepness.

We know we have the worst roads of any county in Oregon. Road levies keep appearing on the ballot and we keep voting them down. Every time this happens our roads get worse. The logic is obvious.

Road levies cause potholes.

Lorraine Eckhard, Documenter of Tillamook County

Her words:

Christmas Day, 1945, my mother was working in the shipyards. We were listening to the radio and they told us to go to the George White Service Center and bring home a couple of servicemen for dinner because they were away from their families. I brought two of them. Ken was one. He was twenty-one and I was seventeen. He made a cute sailor. We were married the following June.

As a child, my brother Charlie and I were sent to the Women's Christian Temperance Union Children's Farm Home, now called Trillium, because my mother had to work and there was no one to take care of us. When he was eight Charlie fell out of a tree and died.

I learned how to work there. We did all our own farming, canning, raised pigs, churned cream into butter. We ate very well. I remember, though we never got hamburgers, meatloaf or ham. There were ten levels of achievement used to encourage good behavior. When anyone got to level ten, they could go have a cigarette with their councilor.

After I grew up and married Ken, we lived in Blaine in one room for four years, had our first kid, and then Ken expanded the house. We had seven kids. Recently, our son Johnny won the filleting contest for the third year in a row at Dory Days. We took deer, gaffed salmon, raised a garden and traded vegetables. I canned a lot of food.

Ken logged for Diamond Lumber, peeled bark, worked the pond, and set choker. Once he followed machinery too close as it went up the hill bending over saplings. One of them snapped up and hit him square in the face. Knocked him silly.

Got hurt setting choker. Haulback line picked him up and dragged him up the hill and threw him off before he got to the drum. He wasn't very safety conscious.

Since then, we ran a dairy. I ran a crew in the broccoli fields, worked in the Hebo Fish Hatchery, fleshed out hides at the mink farm and for ten years made and sold home made bread, thirty-six loaves, twice a week. I've cleaned house, ironed, sewed all the kids' clothes and our square dance costumes.

We've had eighty-five foster kids, twelve at a time in six bedrooms. Many of them come back to visit.

My grandfather was a photographer. I've always liked old pictures. Ken and I took a darkroom class and started our own business. Our advertising motto was, copying old photos is my biz – I get them done in a whiz. I often copied for nothing if I got to keep a copy. That's how I got all these old photographs. I've got hundreds of pictures of Tillamook County, Tillamook, Rockaway, Manzanita, but mostly South County.

Walt Ackley had many photographs of Bay Ocean. I asked him if I could put his pictures in my album and sell them. He gave me all of them. Three days later he died.

I have a whole album of Bay Ocean, the first Tillamook cheese factory right there, near Stillwell St. I have photos on glass negatives and made contact prints of a lot of the old sawmills.

I've given away more old photos than I've sold. There was a fella had a shoe place in Tillamook with a bunch of my pictures on the wall. A woman came in and saw a photograph of a man and a dog by a log truck and she shouts, that's my dad! And that's old Gypper, our dog!

I made a copy of it for her. I've donated my photographs to the museum in my will. If you'd like some, leckhardt@oregoncoast.com, 503-392-3328.

You Can't Handle the Truth

"You can't handle the truth," is a famous movie line uttered by Jack Nicholson playing a cornered General on the stand.

I used to be a liar.

I could say I'm from Texas and it was required, but that's a cheap shot. I felt, I guess, my life wasn't exciting enough and needed help. I had a friend a few years older who told me, in his gentle manner, it's not always necessary to top every story. I felt chagrin. I'm very coachable.

When I tried to stop lying, it was most difficult to tell the truth to myself. Since then, I've developed a taste for it and as Robert, a character in a Hemingway story said, I try not to lie to myself too much.

I heard recently woman's clothing size 8 in 1950 was in 1970 relabeled size 4 and in 2006, size zero. This is rampant in the clothing industry and researchers found improved people's body image. It's called vanity sizing. My father would have called it something else.

I recently ordered a drink and was told there was no size small, only sizes medium and larger. In one experiment, people were given cookies that were labeled either medium or large, and then measured how much they ate. They ate many more cookies labeled medium than large. The cookies were identical.

Most Americans don't realize the soda they order today is six times larger than sodas 60 years ago. Also, a 32-ounce soda at McDonald's is called a large, but the same drink at Wendy's is called a medium. A hamburger today is much larger than it used to be.

One analyst said people often don't have control over their body size and shouldn't feel shame. “It's not a question of being lied to," she said. "It's a question of do we want to be lied to." A double-A bra in the U.S. in Asia is labeled C. Any further comment by me on this subject is above my pay grade.

Lying to oneself is not a recent phenomenon. It was commonly accepted behavior during the time of Beowulf to stand up around the campfire, beat one’s chest and tell everyone how great a warrior you are. You can still see this behavior by fans at NFL games. When Bobby Fischer and Mohammed Ali announced they were the greatest, they were criticized for their lack of humility when they were simply stating a fact. I used to counsel students with self-esteem so low it was a handicap. Almost all artists greatly undervalue their works.

Voting for our political leaders is still one area where we do not want humility. We want someone to tell us they know what to do better than anyone else. We don’t want a partner. We want someone we believe is smarter and braver than we are to pick up the reins of our runaway stagecoach.

Finding an accurate value of our own self worth is difficult, if not impossible, and is probably a fool’s errand. We need to believe in ourselves. If we fudge the truth a bit, then good for us. I also found out recently, according to one study, creative people lie to themselves more often.

Keeping that in mind, this is your nationally known finalist for the Pulitzer, your incisively profound, columnist, Schubert Moore, signing off.

The Way o' Things

Recently we spent a Saturday with other Tillamook County residents at John and Sue Tenny's house, making thirty gallons of sauerkraut. We layered it in big buckets with a little sliced onion, carrot, caraway and salt. We pounded it with big wooden tampers to break down the vegetable cell structure to release the moisture stored inside so the yeast living on all fruits and vegetables could begin it's magic of preserving a food that will keep for years without refrigeration. The kraut needs to ferment at 60°-65° until we stop the natural souring process by canning it.

This isn't news to most Tillamook County residents. Your grandparents probably made kraut. Perhaps, you have. We're a natural people here in our agricultural county, still connected to the earth. But that is not the case in most cities. They have no idea where their food comes from.

I wrote a novel titled Pacific City, published it myself, and sold two hundred copies in a town of five hundred. You can get it on Amazon. A runaway is being taught by a recluse who makes his living hunting and fishing. He tells her:

"I heared stories, people eatin' out at them fast food places all the time. People have forgotten where food a-comes from. They think it's funny about milk a-comin' out of cow's teats. They think meat a-comes in them little white trays a-wrapped in plastic. Well, it don't. They ain't a piece o' meat you put in your mouth without somebody bloodyin' his hands. Every livin' thing eats some other livin' thing, you included. And when your time a-comes, vultures or crabs will eat you unless you're unlucky enough to die in a hospital. Then the germs a-livin' inside you will eat you up just a-leavin' dust and bones. I don't know how old you are. You're a big girl. It's high time you learnt the way o' things."

It's high time we learned there is no such thing as fresh frozen fish, fat-free half-and-half, turkey bacon, boneless ribs, or fresh-from-concentrate juice. We're lying to ourselves. If it doesn't look like a potato, it's not, even if it says so on the frozen french fries box. Ham doesn't need water. When you look at the ingredients, the words for food have few syllables.

When I wanted to help slaughter a lamb we bought I was told I needed therapy. My friend Brenda Charter is raising two pigs named Pork and Beans. We're buying some. I want to understand the food I eat.

Something's wrong. I know because we're close to forty percent obesity and we publish more diet books than any country on earth. We're ranked 38th in life expectancy behind 12th place France which, aside from being the designated smoking country for Europe, drinks alcohol daily, uses butter, the heaviest whipping cream they can find, raw eggs, medium rare hamburgers and vegetables from the produce, not the canned goods aisle. They go to lunch without shopping or multitasking. They sit down. They eat. They talk. It takes them an hour.

The best philosophy for cooking – buy the best ingredients you can afford and do as little to them as possible.

Well, Schubert, I had a friend ask, hands on hips, what do you do if you want to make a pie and peaches aren't in season?

I make apple.

A friend asked me if margarine, rice cakes, turkey bacon, fat-free sour cream and the like will help her live longer.

No, I said, it won't. It will just seem longer.

Theft is Bad

A few weeks ago intrepid HH editor Mary Faith Bell wrote about timber theft. Theft is bad. I was taught in kindergarten, don't take things that don't belong to you. I've experienced theft, both as the thefter and as the theftee. I once ate a chicken salad sandwich and didn't pay for it. With french fries. It wasn't worth it. I'm still thinking about it and publishing my theft in a newspaper seeking absolution from the Walgreen's lunch counter in Dallas, Texas, decades later.

And I've been thefted from. We lived on a corner of a busy street in Portland in a house with no backyard and two side yards. We got a lot of traffic. Someone stole a sprinkler from our front yard. And our lawn furniture. And a marijuana plant.

I know, I know, but it was the sixties. Technically it was the seventies, but you get my point. Somehow someone came into possession of a few marijuana seeds and thought it would be funny to plant them along with a small Doug fir to decorate one of our busy side yards. Both plants did really well. When one plant got to about three feet tall, someone stole it, along with the other one. Maybe they were going to make menthols.

One theft made our friends laugh. We had nine yards of barkdust dumped one Saturday afternoon. I went out after breakfast Sunday morning to spread it around and shortly stood before my wife. Why aren't you spreading the barkdust, she asked. Someone stole it, I said.

I called the police. I told them what happened. I can identify it, I said. It's medium fir.

I don't mean to condone theft, but to steel a tree? That's a lot of work. You have to be in pretty good shape to steal a tree. I doubt if I could steal a full-grown rose bush without hurting myself.

When I first moved fresh from the big city, ignorant of the ways of rural Oregon, I saw a sign that said free wood. Someone was giving away the trees in a too-mature cherry orchard. I thought how neat was that. After I borrowed a chainsaw, rented a trailer, cut up ancient cherry trees in a hard rain and thick mud, loaded the trailer, unloaded the trailer, tried to split the wood and stack it, I didn't think it was all that neat.

Most thieves are quiet while they're stealing, at least they are in the movies. Thieves do a lot of creeping. How can you creep and use a chainsaw? According to Editor Bell's story, no one was allowed to cut trees that time of year in the forest because of fire danger. There is nothing that announces what you're doing or where you are like a chainsaw. It has the same effect as shouting, "Hey! Stealing trees over here!"

What would you do with the wood you don't sell? Would you set your four-year-old on your knee and say, yep, little Johnny, your daddy stole that wood burning in the fireplace?

The Ballad of the One-eyed Old Man and the Kid

Based on a true story

Whether you're young or whether you're old, and despite all the things that you did.

Though the details might change, this is your story, too, the one-eyed old man and the kid.

The wind and the rain, the weather kept changing, birds in flock after flock.

but not in the Sportsman where the one-eyed old man stood silent by the cues like a rock.

In a beautiful bridge, the kid cradled his cue, like a dancer he moved round the floor.

The old man moved slow. His thumb and his finger just couldn't make the bridge anymore.

You shoot a good stick. The kid froze in mid-stroke, looked up, his brow red and hot.

With his head near the table, I've heard about you, said the kid and then sank the shot.

Because of the draw they're not matched early on and the kid never misses a ball.

The old man's game was a little bit off, even though he gave it his all.

He spoke to himself, pull it together. Then realized his advice was all wrong.

Don't try to win. Just sink the next shot and it carried him all contest long.

They finally met in the final two games, the one-eyed old man and the kid.

The kid was in first, the old man behind, in spite of all that he did.

The kid broke the rack and left him a shot and as well as the old man was able,

one shot at a time, one shot at a time, the one-eyed old man ran the table.

In their last game the kid broke and left him a shot. The old man shot and missed badly. He sat down while the kid made ball after ball. The old man shook his head sadly.

The old man could feel the fatigue of the game, three hours of laser-sharp pool.

He knew what was coming, the badly missed shots, another incompetent old fool.

He realized the best of his games were all gone. He'll never be any better than he is.

Once he was good, but just average now. He'll never beat this young whiz.

His body had failed. He'd started the slide. He'll quit 'fore he turns apathetic.

And never again will he be able to beat this young whiz, strong and athletic.

The kid lined up his shot. The eight ball sat poised on the edge of the closest side pocket.

The kid shot way too hard, and before anyone knew, the cue ball had scratched like a rocket.

The one-eyed old man held his cue like an anchor because he could feel himself reel.

The kid came up and held out his hand, and said I know how you feel.

How could you possibly know how I feel, to spend your whole life playing pool

and to lose half your sight. You couldn't possibly know. If you think so I think you're a fool.

You're young and you're fit. You don't know what it's like, in spite of all that you did.

The kid made a shrug. His lips curled a smile. I'm blind in one eye, said the kid.

If you're straight like a kid, if you're lucky, some day, you'll be old, a bent over one.

Just draw a deep breath. Just shoot the next shot and pile up those trips round the sun.

Freedom of Listening

119 journalists were murdered last year for what they wrote. I have a friend who keeps referring to the mainstream media, as if it were a groupthink phalanx of zombies repeating what Big Brother said. Big Brother must have been displeased with their version of his truth.

The main reason I write a humor column is to crack myself up and maybe you, too. However, there is another reason. You can address subjects in a humor column that otherwise might not make it through. I've written of terminal illness, global warming, endangered species, divorce, testosterone, lying to ourselves, homelessness, poverty, and so on. I'm arrogant enough to think I might have something to say you need to hear. I'm not arrogant enough to compare myself with those 119 martyrs to freedom of speech.

Still, I have just a hint of what it might be like. I've received abusive emails in this job. My photo is in the newspaper every week. Locally, everyone recognizes me. People I've never met address me by my first name. I've been censored by my editor when my treatment of gender, prejudice, race or sex she thought too salty for a family newspaper. But my biggest battle is with myself, fighting against self-editing.

A friend said, I know why you write. You want to be famous. Anyone who wants to be famous is a fool. Ask the families of those 119 journalists. I write this column because we like to do things we're good at.

I wonder what it must be like to consider self-editing when someone might put a pistol to the back of my head because of what I've written. Those 119 journalists gave their lives so you could read their version of the truth. The type of binary thinking that labels complex concepts like the myriad reasons journalists write into an either/or category like mainstream media reveals lack of understanding at best, or worst, intellectual laziness. There are just journalists, each as different as you to me. There is no such concept as mainstream media.

When you express your opinion, you're doing exactly what I do. The only difference is the size of the audience. There are places in this world, in this country, actually, where expressing your opinion will bring you harm. You're no stranger to self-editing. You do it automatically, to adjust to your audience, to prevent the young from too much truth, to keep your job, to keep your friends, to stay married.

Still, you have a responsibility to speak out, to express your opinion on important subjects like politics, religion, or lack thereof, education, taxes and so on.

However, you have another responsibility. You have the responsibility to listen, too. I don't mean marking time tapping your foot waiting for the speaker to finish so you can give your opinion, but to really listen. To actively listen. How will we ever learn anything new from each other if we're talking all the time? We need to spend as much time listening as speaking.

Here's a phrase to help you listen –"You're saying," and then repeat what you heard. You'll be amazed how often you heard wrong.

Those 119 journalists wrote what they thought you needed to hear, and they were killed for it. To honor them, let's listen to each other.

Christmas Tale – A True Story

Why do we tell our kids this Santa Claus story? It's a big fat fib and we know we'll eventually get caught. It's our job to teach our kids about the world, so what's going on here?

What are we teaching when we tell this Yule time lie and continue to complicate it with elves, a toy factory at 90° N latitude located on a floating ice sheet which is, by the way, melting, reindeer to pull a sled through the sky, one with a drinker's nose, a Mrs. Claus (Didn't we think Santa's job was complicated enough without a wife?), and a reward and punishment system based on behaviors of children clearly too young to understand it?

And the guy himself? He's addicted to nicotine, sugar, and has a weight problem. Well, at least that part is realistic.

We never did the Santa thing with our kid and he was just fine except for large chunks of his teenage years lost in the caverns of Dungeons and Dragons, so I wouldn't rely on our advice.

I think men made up the Santa tale. Perhaps it's compensation for being caught lying. How could she not have believed really big tires and chrome wheels aren't a safety issue? Or you need the new smart phone for your job? Or you bought a 30.06 to protect your home and children. The scope? You're still working on that.

So when we finally find someone to believe us, usually under six, we really let 'er rip.

I taught seventh grade for years. Twelve-year-olds had already figured out we weren't entirely honest. Marijuana is a gateway drug, to what, Mallomars?

The last day before school recessed for the winter break, middle-schoolers were even more wired than usual, so very little got done. I decided to use that time to teach them how to be a better storyteller. Most people don't realize they use stories all the time on the job. Lawyers take the evidence and construct a story to explain all the facts. Salespeople use stories to link the product and the customer. Can't you feel the wind in your hair with the top down on this baby?

I explained telling a good story uses details and the senses. I demonstrated by telling the story of how I learned about Santa, and then asked for volunteers.

One girl came forward to sit on the story stool at the front of class. She had absorbed what I tried to teach and told a detailed story of her mother taking her little sister and her to the beach, their favorite place to go. They rented a house. It was storming outside with big waves crashing. The mother fixed fragrant cups of hot chocolate, which they drank in front of a hearth fire. They ate their favorite dinner, gooey mac and cheese and for dessert, their favorite, vanilla ice cream on warm cinnamon cake.

Then the mother said, I have something to tell you. There isn't a Santa Claus. I buy the presents.

The girls were shocked. Really, the two little girls asked in disbelief? There isn't a Santa? Nope, the mother said. No Santa.

The two sisters tried to take it in. What about the Easter Bunny?

Nope. No bunny, the mother said. I hide the eggs.

The girls were rattled.

What about the tooth fairy? Nope. While you're sleeping I take the tooth and put the money there.

The girls were stunned, wide-eyed with too much truth.

The mother figured she was on a roll and might as well clear the decks.

And that guy who lives with us? He's not your father.

Should April 15 Be January 1?

January 1 is not the beginning of anything. It's hard to pick a date for a beginning of the new year. It would make some kind of sense for the new year to begin on the winter solstice, December 21, since the days become longer, but only for only those in the northern hemisphere. South of the equator, the days become shorter.

The new year could begin in September since kids start school in a new grade. But all that's changed too. Some begin in August. Some actually never stop going. Some are in multi-grades. Some are homeschooled.

I always thought we could begin the new year when the salmon returned, but that varies with each river and what do we do with Kansas?

We use a calendar by Pope Gregory, even though some of us aren't Catholic. The Roman Calendar uses the same date, and they have a lot more options for worship. I always liked Jupiter. There was no misunderstanding him. If he didn't like what you were doing, ZAP! with the lightning bolt.

We could have a year that lasts 1461 days to begin every four trips around the sun at the beginning of the Olympic Games or the World Cup. You know the World Cup? Soccer? Since we play soccer now, or our kids do, it's one event the whole world has in common. Business pretty much shuts down during the World Cup so we could all party for that week.

According to Luke 2:21, we celebrate the New Year on Jan. 1 because of the circumcision of Jesus on the eighth day after his birth, when he was named. The fact that he wasn't born on Dec. 25 is beside the point. That date has since gone global. Do you think every single religion knows this?

New Year used to be March 25, Lady's Day, after Jesus' mother, very close to Easter, the first Sunday after the first Monday after the vernal equinox. If we chose Easter for New Year, we could simply be informed by someone who understands when it will be. Businesses begin their new year, called their fiscal year, July 1, if they got any fiscal left. The British Empire used to celebrate New Year on April 1, Tax Day. We could do that, April 15 when any hope for getting ahead that year comes to an end and we drag ourselves into the next year.

But who am I kidding? New Years doesn't have anything to do with Jesus or his mom or longer days or business. It's all about a computerized lighting system of 32,000 LED light bulbs and an outer surface consisting of 504 triangle-shaped crystal panels.

It's the Times Square Ball in New York City. Yearly at 11:59 p.m. EST on December 31, the ball is lowered 77 feet down a specially designed flagpole to signal the start of the new year. It's watched by more than a billion people.

It's a symbol. What does it symbolize? It symbolizes that globally, what with genocides, with predator drones and data mining, with the sexualization of minors (Justin Bieber is still in training wheels) with Marco Rubio already starting the 2016 Presidential campaign in Iowa, with Iran reassuring us their nuclear program is designed only to produce glow-in-the-dark watch dials, with the end of Twinkies and the Ducks remembering how to lose, with the fact you can't even remember your last New Year's resolution, that once again, we dropped the ball.

Poignant – Causes and First Loves

You've been thinking about becoming more involved in a cause that means a lot to you. Maybe it's the homeless in our county, the backpack program to feed kids, adopt-a-family during the holidays, cleaning up our rivers, ocean reserves, the Territorial Sea Plan, politics or fixing our roads. Your cause is like your first love, poignant, bitter and sweet.

Poignant is that scene in Casablanca when of all the gin joints in all the towns in all the world, Ingrid Bergman walks into Humphrey Bogart's saloon after leaving him years before standing at the train station reading a note in the rain that said she wasn't coming. We lose a lot of memories that fall out of our head while we're sleeping, but we keep poignant. Almost any scene in Casablanca is poignant. That's why we're still watching it.

You have to have loved only once to know poignant, the two of you breathing together, when there was ecstasy in every breath you drew. And then you wait for the call that never comes, that day when your heart cracked in two.

You can remember whether it was raining or the day was illuminated with sunlight. You can remember what you were wearing. The pain was so hard and went in so deep it left you with a comical look on your face because your insides had been kicked out.

There's something about this time of year. The fundamental things apply as time goes by. We take a mental inventory at year's end, round up the usual suspects and think, oh, well, one out, one in.

And the music. Why does there always have to be music? It was your song, the song that you listened to together, so that just a few notes can spiral you back into that moment in a heartbeat. A kiss is just a kiss, a sigh is just a sigh, but not if it was your kiss. It was the universe. Play it again.

You walk around with it inside, that memory. It's yours. It will always be yours, reminding you forever of what you were and the surprise of what you've become. Often you're busy and the name recedes for a time. Then an ending comes, like year's end, and you hear another song, should old acquaintance be forgot and never brought to mind, and the name is at your lips.

In the movie Bogart gave up Bergman for a cause bigger then they are. It happens to us as we mature. Love isn't love until you give it away.

We have so much love to give, a person can't hold it all. We yearn for a cause like they had. We're hard wired to do it, to build something larger than we are. That's why we fight so hard for what we believe in, vets and church and schools and battered women and abused kids and the hungry and the homeless and abandoned animals and on and on. It's rare to find anyone who doesn't believe in a cause bigger than themselves.

Contrary to what some philosophers tell us, there aren't kinds of love. Love is love. We bond with another to transcend ourselves. So it is with a cause. We lose ourselves in order to become something greater, and it is bitter and sweet.

So take up your cause. Stand up for what's right. It's a case of do or die, that no one can deny. If you don't get involved, you'll regret it, maybe not today, maybe not tomorrow, but soon and for the rest of your life. Welcome back to the fight. Here's looking at you, Kid.

Fetal Monitors and 4Runners

You may not be able to tell if you've been reading my columns, but I have ethics. I would not, for instance, force my political views on you, despite the fact I'm right and your so wrong your vote should be given to someone more responsible, like, well, me. I would not criticize your religion, sexual practices, or position on gun control and I certainly wouldn't, just because I have a column and you don't, blatantly use it to brag about my new grandson Will, born 7 lbs., 12 oz. with black hair so cute he looks like he's already had his first haircut.

I would use this column, however, to alert you to a barbaric practice now in use in the hospitals using a device resembling something you might see in a museum of torture devices designed in 1400. It's called the fetal spiral electrode. Wait until the CIA sees this "medical instrument." They'll be lining up to trade in their waterboards.

The wrapper for this device says it's "for use on patients requiring fetal heart rate monitoring, by way of fetal scalp, during labor."

In case you're not following, this monitoring device is attached during labor, before the defenseless little baby has even been born. How, you might be asking yourself, do they do that?

They screw it into the baby's head!

In the diagram the tip of this thing looks suspiciously like an upholstery pin, you know, the spiral, needle-pointed wire with a plastic button on top women use to attach covers to the La-Z-Boy to protect the arms from cheese dip? How do I know it's women? Have you ever seen a man use an upholstery pin?

The instructions advise, “Push the Grip back until the spiral tip contacts the presenting part.” What, you might be asking yourself, is the presenting part? It was little Will Moore’s sweet head! “Turn it clockwise one full turn until mild resistance. WARNING: Do not over-rotate.” You think! I’m feeling queasy.

Now, you’re probably asking yourself, what does this have to do with $40,000 baby incubators and Toyota 4Runners?

According to a posting on engadget.com, a lot of babies die in developing nations due to lack of incubators, you know, those heating units that keep baby chickens and humans warm? Used incubators are often donated, as new ones cost about $40,000 each. Often lacking either the technicians or the parts to fix them, however, most of the incubators don't work.

Enter Dr. Jonathan Rosen of Boston University's School of Management, who's ingeniously devised an incubator out of the abundant Toyota 4Runners found in developing nations. Apparently, if you want your nation to develop, you first have to get a bunch of Toyota 4Runners. Rosen cobbled together an incubator using headlights as the heating source, the filters for air purification and the door alarm for emergency notification. The resulting incubator costs about $1,000 to make and can be repaired by auto mechanics. (I would like to see Dr. Rosen’s job description, the part where it says teach students to become managers and oh, by the way, invent incubators.)

I’m writing an email right now to Dr. Rosen (I know, wrong kind of doctor) to ask him to find another way to attach a heart monitor to a baby. If he can cannibalize a 4Runner to make an incubator, he could do this job in his sleep.

Little Will has had a couple bumpy days, heart rate too high and not exactly stable, but he's okay. My heart rate might be too high, too, if somebody attached a monitor to the top of my head using an upholstery pin.

Sand Lake is Funnier Than You Think

For the first half of my life, I tried to be cool. For the second half, I've tried to be funny. Funny is easier. See photo.

Republicans are funnier than Democrats but don't know it. Democrats mean to be funny, but they're too busy laughing at Republicans, like in the comics when the guy in a top hat steps on a banana peel. If that isn't funny, you're a Republican.

Sometimes funny is easy, like the Sand Lake Rules for Riding Off-Highway Vehicles, OHV's, you know, those four-wheel motorcycles that run up and down sand dunes?

Funny is unexpected. To begin with, Sand Lake isn't a lake. It's an estuary. Unexpected. See? Already funny. Over the years the elements wore down some of The Cascade Mountains, and they ended up at Sand Lake. If you were a mountain, right now you'd be laughing so hard you'd be holding your boulders.

If you want to ride at Sand Lake first get an OHV Education Card. Like, that's going to happen. That's what you would do if you're a female. If you're male, the first thing you're going to do is buy enough OHV's, trailer, and RV's to equal the cost of college for your kids. We're not to the funny part yet.

After you've spent all this money, you find you can't just go to the beach and ride the sand the way God meant you to. In Oregon, you can ride in two designated areas, Sand Lake and Oregon Dunes. Remember, the rules say, in addition to the OHV permit, the Siuslaw National Forest also requires recreation permits for campgrounds and day-use staging areas. You probably don't think this is funny, either. The rest of us do, but then we haven't spent $200K.

We probably should mention curfew. It's safe to say you're not going to be riding before 6:00 a.m., but after midnight and that tenth beer and the moon's out, the temptation to ride along the beach is great, which is how much the fine is.

Campers in dispersed areas must have and use a portable toilet. Think about it. No, let's not.

Sound levels at Sand Lake are 97 decibels and since ear damage doesn't start until 100 that gives you three decibels to play with, considerably louder than the blender making your margaritas.

Oops. No booze allowed at Sand Lake. Really stiff fines. Isn't this a riot? I know, what's the point then? Of course you can do what some riders do, get tanked on the way there. Also, you can use a travel coffee mug, because I often hear police officers say, why, he can't be drinking alcohol because it's a coffee mug. You can drink heavily on the way home. Maybe that's why on Sunday nights trying to get to my house alive is like playing a video game where I'm supposed to miss the zigzagging caravans.

Some of the most common violations are no helmets under age 18, with chinstrap.

Let's just pause here and insert some OHV blog postings:

kamakazee – I've heard if you aren't careful you can get hurt at Sand Lake. A guy I knew that worked for the sheriff's department says they have one decapitation a year usually. My boss' wife was on jury duty and the defendant had jumped his Bronco onto a guy riding an OHV. Landed right on top of him. Didn't have a chance.

dirtmama59 – Got to be careful out there. Now if I just had more HORSEPOWER!!!

We're to the funny part. During a decapitation, does the chin strap really matter?

County Commissioners Should Sue Us

Recently the Chinese government said it will enforce a law permitting parents to sue their children if they don't visit them often enough. What a great idea. I have a few more suggested lawsuits.

Parents should also be able to sue their children when they reach teenage years for an acutely developed sense of self-righteousness when they discover their parents are not perfect and feel the need to point out every instance of hypocrisy.

Parents should also be able to sue their children for excessive use of eye rolls and creaky voice (ask your teenage daughter). Parents should also be able to sue their children for their attitude of, if you want to know what's going on in my life, text me.

Children should be able to sue parents for monitoring their Facebook page. Children should also be able to sue parents for leaving dorky messages on their Facebook page.

Why limit law suits to parents and children? Tillamook County Commissioners Josi, Labhart, and Baertlein are supposed to maintain infrastructure. They should be able to sue the voters for not giving them the money to fix the roads.

The residents of Tillamook County should be able to sue the weatherman for lack of winter weather variety. Tillamook county should be able to sue NASA for looking for water on Mars when we've got plenty here. South County should be able to sue North County for having more cachet.

The gun owner who lost his pistol in the Coliseum Theater and found by two children should be able to sue the press for making such a big deal out of it.

Dairy cattle should be able to sue dairy owners after seven years of producing milk for lack of a retirement pasture.

SOLV, Stop Oregon Litter and Vandalism, volunteers trying to keep our beaches and rivers clean, should be able to sue salmon fishers for the innumerable styrofoam bait containers washed up on shore and riverside.

The Energy Industry should be able to sue Oregon coastal counties for making the approval process so cumbersome for siting just off shore, forty-story electricity-generating windmills with lights on top.

The NRA should be able to sue lawmakers because gun owners are having difficulty getting their hands on silencers, which are necessary, as the NRA states, to protect children's hearing.

Two convicted bank robbers should be able to sue the FBI for lack of a rope which made it necessary for them to risk life and limb escaping from a high-rise jail in downtown Chicago by lowering themselves twenty stories using bed sheets.

Brussels sprout farmers should be able to sue the government for the asparagus farmers' bailout.

The Pennsylvania governor should be able to sue NCAA over Sandusky sanctions – oh, wait, that one's been done.

The Ohio electorate should be able to sue Rep. Steven LaTourette for making sense when he told his colleagues, "We should not approve a package put together by a bunch of sleep-deprived octogenarians on New Year's Eve."

The Ducks should be able to sue the Beavers because even though the Ducks beat the Beavers regularly, scarf up all the good football players and are ranked nationally, the Beavers still have an unreasonable number of loyal fans.

I should be able to sue my sisters for making me feel guilty for moving to Oregon.

I should be able to sue my wife for being right so often and when I'm finally right I still have to apologize.

Gary's Gift

I had a dory boat I launched into the surf at Pacific City. It was more than a ton of wood and fiberglass with a steel propeller that could sever a limb. Sometimes it was eight-foot surf traveling fast, seawater weighing in at a ton per square yard. Most launches are easy, but sometimes it took all I had.

At first, I went out by myself. There was no one I disliked enough to risk their life because I was at the helm. As I gained more confidence, I began to take others. My next-door neighbor Gary became my first mate.

Gary is a worrier, and he comes by it honestly. We were having a friendly argument once, and I said, you're a little paranoid about this, Gare. He responded, hell, yeah, I'm paranoid. I take medication for it.

Did I top off the oil, did I fasten the cowling, did I put the plugs in, did I get the bait? He worried over me endlessly. I had offers from other dorymen for Gary.

He told me once, I started to call you pretty early this morning about the oil level. What time was that, Gare? Three a.m. I thought you'd probably be asleep so I didn't. Good decision, Gare.

I'm not sure when Gary moved from neighbor to friend. It was more than that, when I realized he would lay down his life for me in a heartbeat without thought.

Things change when that happens. As skipper, I now had the added responsibility to never put us anywhere near that situation. I know what you're thinking. A skipper should always think that way, but that's not what I'm talking about. Cary would have put himself in danger for me the same way I would for my children. It's different and it's humbling.

Gary built the Fremont Bridge in Portland. Not by himself, of course. He had help, but, yes, he was one of those, forty stories up before safety gear, on an eight-inch beam that wobbled when he walked on it because he hadn't put the other bolt in it yet, looking down over the Willamette River to see seagulls flying below him.

I'm making a poor job of telling you what I'm trying to say. He took my word as the cold stone truth. If dories weren't going out and he asked me what I thought, and I said we could make it, Gary got in the boat and that was the end of it. There are some in this town that would say that was poor judgment on Gary's part. In our defense, in thirteen years my dory never flipped or swamped and a lot of dorymen in this town can't say that.

For someone to obey without question, to trust you in their heel bones is a gift and allows one to mature in a way not possible without that kind of trust.

Even though I sold the dory, Gary is still the same, worrying over me. If I don't put the garbage can out on Tuesday, he calls. If he thinks something's not right, he calls.

There is only one time Gary got on my nerves. We had been tuna fishing forty-two miles out and were making the trip back, running fast with Evenstar dory, high on adrenaline and wave spray and three hundred pounds of albacore, when we broke down half-way home. Charles Loos made a bridal, hooked us up and started, at seven miles an hour, towing us the twenty-one miles back, a three-hour cruise.

After an hour, I turned to Gary and said, if you sing the theme song to Gilligan's Island one more time I'm going to throw you overboard.

Mr. News Guy Explains Political Correctivity

It's time once again for Mr. News Guy to explain to you the mysteries of language and how to talk good, specifically, how not to be politically non-incorrect. If you're here to learn when to use popular words like killer, sweet, raw, sick, choice and bad, you're at the wrong column. If you're here to learn when to use nifty and far out, I'm sorry to inform you, John Denver died in 1997.

Hidden in these politically correct (PC) phrases, of course, are many contradictions. How can bad and all good mean the same, as does Uber (German), Kosher (Jewish), Primo (Italian) and Wicked (Disney)?

The Swedish have generously offered to help us out of the politically incorrect jungle regarding gender-neutral personal pronouns, even though we hardly know each other. They have Han for masculine He, Hon for feminine Her (I already see a problem there), and have generously offered Hen for both male and female. I'm sure my wife would approve because I know hen.

Now off-limits is Holding Down the Fort, offensive to Native Americans, since we all know whom the fort was being held down against. Handicap is also off limits from the disabled reference, and can be offensive to beggars, as in with cap in hand. Christmas already under siege will be joined by Happy Holidays because it originated from holy in holidays. You're also not allowed Xmas because X is the Greek letter 'chi,' representing the first two letters of Christ. The favored word substitute for prayer is now thoughts, as in keep hen in your thoughts.

The word English is not permitted because of the dominance of the English language worldwide and is looked upon as linguistic imperialism or Western Hegemony. Hegemonies are PC unless they block your neighbor's view.

Whatever do we do with OMG and butt monkey, as in I will not be the butt monkey to further ridicule? OMG is okay because it isn't technically a prayer, but butt monkey just sounds dirty and so best to avoid.

Twitterverse is PC unless combined with one of the Kardashians, the mixture of which renders it toxic.

One must be very careful with the phrase, Not Too Black (see definition below, Not Too White).

Not Too White (see Not Too Black).

China Takes Over The World is permitted if spoken with a bow (previously, Japan Takes Over The World, but Japan found it couldn't afford it.)

If you're from south of the Mason-Dixon Line, you may say almost anything and avoid being politically incorrect if you add, bless your heart, as in, I heard one of your parents was a mule, bless your heart.

Apocalypse, Frankenstorm, Obamagedden, God Particle, Rogue Nukes, Near Earth Asteroid, any one of which may wipe out all life as we know it on our planet, are all politically correct if pronounced properly.

Dutch Treat is possibly offensive to the Dutch, since it portrays them as either (take your choice) thrifty (good) or stingy (bad) (See also Scottish/Jewish)

Global Warming is not PC, but Climate Change is, although this probably makes little difference to you if you have a polar bear shedding in your swimming pool.

It is still politically correct to use master/slave computer jargon to describe the editor/columnist relationship.

Hipster is not PC if you're over thirty. Hipsters are often spotted wearing vintage thrift-store-inspired fashions, slim-fit jeans and thick-rimmed glasses flaunting their swag. It is not PC to flaunt your swag unless your swag is way hotter and renders you a hipster. If you're over seventy, hipster is PC, since having come around again, you're grandfathered in.

Liking on Facebook or other websites is PC if you're a dull sheep who wouldn't know an original thought if it bit you on your swag.

It's never PC to use fracking in mixed company.

Laughter Means You're Not Going to Kill Me

When I was a teen, I read that feature in Readers Digest, a small, fat magazine found now only in doctors' offices. It was a collection of condensed anecdotes that were supposed to make you chuckle.

I heard recently Readers Digest doesn't have much longer. They didn't make the transfer to the digital age. Does that mean eventually there will be no reading materials in your dentist's office? Will you find a stack of digital readers with Sunset Magazine downloaded on them or will Dr. Thompson expect you to bring your own iPad or smart phone?

You'll have to bring your own humor. Laugh and the whole world laughs with you. You become human when you laugh at yourself, which is why Donald Trump is an alien.

I was on my daily errands in Pacific City, which includes the post office. I started around a blind corner and suddenly confronted a man. He looked at me for ½ second, dropped his eyes, said, just picking up my mail, and laughed, heh, heh, heh.

Have you noticed we laugh when nothing's funny? We laugh all the time. Sorry, didn't mean to bump you, hee, hee. Ha, I grabbed the wrong item, Ho, ho, ho, Merry Christmas.

Thomas Carlyle said, only humans laugh, but Tom should have spent more time with chimpanzees. When chimps are scuffling and another chimp approaches, one of the chimps will make a breathy, rapid, exhalation, a sort of pant, pant. pant. This is the precursor to our ha, ha, ha. This signals to others we're not really fighting. It diffuses tension, reduces conflict and makes our lives safer. Actually I think all of us should spend more time with chimpanzees.

The man I nearly ran into at the post office was telling me, I'm no threat, so let me pass in peace. That's why John Wayne said, you better smile when you call me that, Pilgrim.

Laughter releases endorphins, a natural painkiller, the same as running, chocolate, or sex, but with your street clothes on. Making someone else laugh is almost as good as laughing. This explains tickling, stand-up and William Shatner.

Mice laugh. A researcher was rubbing mice with the tip of his finger. Rather than run away, the mice would chase his finger about and press themselves against it. Wondering if they were laughing but he just couldn't hear, he recorded them at 50K/cycles/sec (humans hear up to 20K) slowed it down and played it back. Hee, hee, hee the mice went, they're little legs clawing the air, his fingertip scratching their stomachs. My father was so ticklish he couldn't bear to watch us kids wash our feet.

The third type of laughter comes from tragicomedy, represented for millennia by the drama masks of Dionysus, one laughing, one crying. This symbolized his dual nature, or who gets the pie in the face. Me falling off a cliff is tragedy. *You* falling off a cliff is comedy. Comedy is tragedy after a bathroom break.

Occasionally grieving is mistaken for laughter. The face behaves the same – bared teeth, tears, howls. Expecting one thing and getting another creates comedy or tragedy. Grandpa is a woman is either comic, tragic, or a country-western song. And then there is the language – a comic claims, they laughed until they cried. I *killed* last night.

At the highest level of humor is the biggest joke. You want to live. You're going to die. Isn't that a riot? Whether you decide to laugh or cry about it is the most important decision you will ever make. You might as well laugh. You can't *do* anything about it. It also determines if people still think you're funny after you've forgotten to bring the potato chips.

So Carlyle got it wrong. Other animals laugh. Perhaps the only valid quote about humankind's uniqueness is what Mark Twain said. Man is the only animal that blushes – or has reason to.

We Have Too Much Nature

We have too much nature in our county. Take the moon, for instance. One morning recently I woke way too early wondering, did I leave a light on? No. The moon was shining right in my eyes. And this isn't the first time, either. Has anyone noticed this seems to happen about once a month?

Also, too much wind. My neighbors have weather stations to tell them the wind speed. They watch their weather stations as much as TV. We don't have a weather station. Instead, we put up a windsock. If the wind comes from the north, good weather, from the south, rain, east, it gets cold. From the west, no one has figured that out, yet. We look at the windsock and say, rain today, and it rains.

Why don't you get a weather station, my neighbor Carol asked? I replied, if I need to know the wind speed, I can just call you. I used to call and say, what was the wind speed last night, Carol? She would tell me and we would chat. Over the years the conversation has truncated. My phone rings. I pick it up. Seventy-two, Carol says, and hangs up.

I have no reason to know the wind speed. No one calls and asks, so, Schubert, what was the wind speed last night? If they did, I'd say, call Carol.

Also, too much rain. I don't want to complain about the rain, but people in the rain. Actually, it's my sister's complaint. My sister came to visit from Texas. She looked out the window at the rain. Kids were playing soccer. She had a puzzled look on her face. Don't they know it's raining, she said? One of the first things I bought when I moved to Oregon in the Jurassic era was an umbrella. Boy, that was stupid. I went out in the rain and opened it up. Passersby shook their head and thought, out-of-stater or brain damage.

Yesterday I saw a guy walking along, no hat, smoking a cigarette in the rain. Did I think, mental defective who doesn't know enough to come in out of the rain? No. I thought, Oregonian.

Another indicator of too much nature? Deer. Mrs. Green agrees. Mrs. Green likes to grow roses since they grow much bigger in Oregon than they ever did in Missouri. In Missouri, she watered, trained, fertilized, fed, sprayed, pruned and they would fit in a small teacup. In Oregon, if you ignore them they will grow to the size of dinner plates. Mrs. Green was in heaven. Until she came out one morning with pruning shears and no roses. The deer had eaten them all. Over the next few months, it was sad to see Mrs. Green become obsessed with deer the way Ahab was with his white whale. She put up fences the deer thought were fun to jump over. She spread deer repellant around her yard. They didn't seem to mind the smell, but I quit visiting. One day I went to deliver some rose catalogues and when I got out of the car I was hit in the face with a stream from a motion-sensor water cannon the deer thought was fun to play in.

My neighbor Bob likes to hunt deer. On one trip he came back skunked and had to wait to pull into his drive so six deer could cross the street in front of him to go into his yard to eat his flowers. When Mrs. Green heard this story, she pleaded for Bob to come to her yard to hunt deer.

My conclusion? Too much nature. Mrs. Green would agree. If you don't get your deer, Mrs. Green invites you to bring your 30.06 and hunt in her front yard.

Or she would if she were still here. She went back to Missouri. Smaller roses, but less nature.

Get Back in the Box

Recently I did not attend a workshop conducted by the President of the United States of America for Tillamook County times three. See, if you look at our county as if it were the United States of America, the chief executive would be the President, right? But Tillamook County calls our chief executive, commissioner, and instead of one, we have three of them, Commissioners Josi, Labhart and Baertlein, or Commissioner Jablein for short. Think three Obamas. Or maybe you wouldn't like to think about three Obamas.

The acronym CPAC stands for community planning advisory committee. Many communities in Tillamook County have a CPAC. Just think of CPAC's like our congress, only uncapitalized. They relay your opinions to Commissioner Jablein, only Tillamook's CPAC's, or our congress, has a higher approval rating than Our Congress, capitalized, in Washington D.C., which when I last checked was rated below root canals and cow poop.

Commissioner Jablein is pretty happy he doesn't have something President Obama does have, Our Congress. Instead of Commissioner Jablein having Our Congress, he has our congress, meaning- he's pretty much free to do whatever he'd like. I'll bet President Obama would be pretty happy to trade jobs with Commissioner Jablein some days. He'd also be willing to trade Our Congress for our congress.

Since I didn't go to the workshop, it was pretty confusing. I had to listen to an hour and a half recording of the meeting and sometimes it was hard to tell who was saying what. I had to have help from friends who were at the meeting. You wouldn't think it would be much fun sitting around listening to an hour and a half recording of Commissioner Jablein and our congress, but it was actually pretty entertaining.

The people at the meeting sounded pretty confused. Even Commissioner Jablein sounded confused. What was confusing him was the box. Our congress kept getting out of it.

When our congress got out of the box they kept giving Commissioner Jablein their opinions and expected him to appreciate it. I got the impression Commissioner Jablein wasn't entirely pleased with our congress being out of the box and kept trying to get them back in it, because he kept saying, you're out of the box. Commissioner Jablein thought our congress was supposed to be giving their opinions to CAC's, community action committees which haven't existed in a couple of decades, but our congress kept trying to skip the nonexistent CAC's and give their opinions to Commissioner Jablein until he told our congress they were out of the box, that they didn't exist and in fact had never existed. I told you it was confusing.

I think Commissioner Jablein hurt our congress' feelings. One member of our congress, Larry Rouse, told me it was humiliating, to be told he never existed, and to receive not so much as a thank you, to just be dismissed after giving up his Saturday mornings or Monday evenings once a month for seven years going to two-hour meetings so our congress could relay what Tillamook County residents had on their mind. Sean Carlton, a member of our congress, sounded hurt. "You mean we never existed?" Sean Carlton asked. Nope, Commissioner Jablein said. Never existed.

Since then Commissioner Jablein has changed his mind. I don't know what happened to change his mind but now he believes our congress does exist. In fact Commissioner Jablein said, I have a whole new appreciation of our congress.

I would like to know what changed his mind. Maybe it was the reaction of the Tillamook County residents who didn't appreciate being told our congress didn't exist. Or maybe Commissioner Jablein reflected on some of what our congress had told him, and thought, you know, our congress has some pretty good ideas. Yeah, I'll bet that's what changed his mind. Reflection.

And, Commissioner Jablein must have also reflected, things could be worse. Instead of our congress, he could have Our Congress.

I Need a Media Manager

The Target store chain is hiring a media manager. I need a media manager. My story's not getting out. I'm told I can use only 140 characters.

Sometimes my wife Joani and I argue. Our most recent argument was about the birdseed. We had a forty-pound sack of black-oil sunflower seeds the mice had gotten into. I put the sack into a plastic bucket to protect it from the mice. See? Responsible behavior.

Joani wanted the trail of birdseed swept up. I did, but she said I missed some. If I had a media manager, he would have sent her a tweet explaining the only birdseed I missed was mixed in with a pile of lumber and it wasn't really birdseed any more, anyway. It was birdseed husks. The mice had already eaten the seeds and left the husks. He would have said the mice were no longer interested in the birdseed husks so there was no need to pick up the pile of wood pieces and sweep up the birdseed husks. See? Faultless logic.

Joani is immune to faultless logic. For instance, I tried to explain to her the birdseed husks were in the garage and that was my area. If there had been birdseed husks in the living room, I would have swept them up, probably. At least after she pointed them out to me. She had the whole house. I just had the garage and if I wanted to leave a couple of birdseed husks lying about in some lumber, it should be okay. I had no luck with that explanation. Maybe a media manager could have gotten my story out.

Another time I could use a media manager is with my children. They have started to explain things to me in a loud voice using single syllables. Then they pause and make eye contact. That's exactly the way I treat the elderly.

Once my son Patrick was teasing me and I said, did I ever tell you, you were adopted? That should have shut him up, I thought. Instead, he fired back, you don't know what a relief that is to find out. His wife said, well, Honey, how long have you had that one in the holster? They laughed a lot. See? If I had a media manager, I would have won that exchange.

There was one day I could really have used a media manager. My son Josh and his wife M'lissa and their new daughter were coming to visit. They didn't arrive when we expected them. Hours went by. I became more and more upset. It was dark when they finally showed up.

I told them how angry and disappointed I was. Without realizing it, I was using my outside voice. When I finished, my daughter-in-law was crying.

And then the most amazing thing happened. I heard my son Josh quietly and in a calm, reasonable voice explain to M'lissa what I really meant. What I really meant was I had been worried sick about them, that I imagined they had broken down or worse, had a car accident with the baby in the car, that I didn't mean all those harsh things I had said, that what I meant was aside from my wife, there was no one in the world I loved more.

I realized I had a media manager. He was my son and he did a much better job of explaining what I meant than I could have. I wondered when it was my son had grown into this wise man. As my media manager, maybe he could explain to his mother why I shouldn't have to sweep up the birdseed husks.

I think it might take him more than 140 characters.

I'm Not the Darth Vader of Birddom

Let's just get this out front right now – I don't like birds.

I know, I know. Everybody likes birds. I'm a writer and a lot of my friends are scientists and birders, so I want some sympathy here. My friend Dave can ID a bird while sleeping. Dave, not the bird. Once Dave was trying to show me buffalo heads. Buffleheads, he corrected. But I couldn't see them. Where! I asked, exasperated. I can't see them. There's something in the way. The things in the way, Dave said, his temples tightening, are the buffleheads.

I'll tell you who else doesn't like birds. Dairymen. I had a female dairyman tell me through gritted teeth the birds crap (can I say crap in the newspaper?) in the feed and the cows get sick. Birding and Blues, she said, (we have the Birding and Blues Festival here where a bunch of adults in expensive hiking gear and 1500 power binoculars fawn over birds.) my idea of Birding and Blues, she said, would be to listen to some good blues music while killing every bird in the area. Her eyes sort of glittered.

I have two categories of birds, little brown birds, sometimes yellow, and big birds. Often birders mistake hummingbirds for birds, when actually they're a species of large winged cockroach. Don't believe me? Google it.

My wife Joani loves birds. We have a spring-loaded feeder that let's one category of birds, her favorites, little brown birds, eat the birdseed and other birds, by which Joani means blue jays, go hungry. What do you have against blue jays, I ask, in an on-going and losing bird argument we've been having for fifteen years? Stellar jays, she says smugly, holding her bird book by Roger Tory Peterson, the Obi-Wan Kanobi of birddom. They're birds, I say. This is a bird feeder. They deserve birdseed, too, right?

No, they don't, Joani says. They're rude.

I'm not sure how I got roped into an argument about bird etiquette behavior? I mean, what I learned in that famous documentary, Jurassic Park, are that birds are direct descendants of velociraptors and would pick your eyes out to put in their martinis if you lay still long enough. During my earlier party days, I did lie still long enough and I woke to see a bird eyeing my eyes. (No, that's not how I lost my eye, but it could happen.)

I was out for a walk on the mudflats at Sand Lake. A guy was digging sand shrimp for salmon fishing. He had a piece of string tied around one foot. The other end was tied around the neck of a sea gull. He'd dig some shrimp, put them in his bucket, and kick the sea gull. Dig, put shrimp in the bucket, kick the sea gull. A state police officer walked up and asked him what he was doing. I'm protecting my sand shrimp, he said. This gull was stealing them. Did you know these birds are protected, the police officer asked? I *am* protecting them. I'm using this one as an example so the others will leave my sand shrimp alone so I won't have to kill them. You are so busted, the police officer said.

Once my next-door neighbor Gary was helping me wire an electric fence to keep the raccoons away from the birdseed and I said, Gare, what if the fence electrocutes the very birds we're trying to feed? Oh, Schubert, Gary said with infinite patience and great wisdom gathered over the years, there are lots of birds. Good point, Gare.

It's Better to Light One Candle

We don't have enough synergy in Tillamook County according to an article by fine HH staff writer Joe Wrabeck about a Tourism Symposium held in Tillamook recently. Synergy is one of those words the average person doesn't use but always means to, to show we're educated.

Synergy means the answer is greater than the sum of its parts. 1+1=2, I was taught in my math group at Roger Q. Mills Elementary School in Texas. With synergy, 1+1=3. If I had put 1+1=3 in my arithmetic workbook, I would never have gotten into the Blue Birds, the group I wanted in, from the group I was in, the Albatrosses. Texans believe in rugged individualism. They frown on synergy.

According to Wrabeck, the reason we need synergy is to get tourism money. The article claimed people with tourism money to spend, head to Clatsop County to the north or Lincoln County below and then drive back and forth skipping Tillamook County, creating a veritable money freeway.

Tillamook County's strategy is to slow them down long enough to leave some money here. I thought our roads would have done the trick. Most of that, though, goes to tire dealers and auto repair shops, which, I guess, is a kind of synergy.

The main ideas thrown around in the symposium was to get tourist money by creating synergy with water trails kayakers might use, lighthouses, and the Quilt Trails, giant wooden quilt representations nailed to the front of dairy barns, I don't know how many lighthouse-viewing, quilting kayakers there are out there, but that sounds like a pretty narrow market to me. I have a friend who might qualify, but she's gay. Her partner spent most of her time recently filling out her March Madness brackets, so she's not a candidate.

I have a few suggestions for creating synergy. The Tillamook County Creamery Association could synergize with the Tillamook Transportation District. Since milk trucks are going to dairies all over the county anyway, they could drag a trailer with seating. The customers could view the Quilt Trail while they're waiting for the milk truck to fill.

Since we live in a fishing destination county and with the growing concern about healthful diets, a natural result would be creating synergy with a sushi restaurant and bait shop.

I tried using this strategy on my wife Joani, but she's immune to synergy. Granted it was still in the test phase, but when I tried combining tasks like washing the dishes and the car, she was not synergetic. She said, only *your* clothes, when I suggested synergizing showering and the laundry.

Another opportunity for synergy would the obvious one for our county. Dairymen have gone to Sweden to visit plants that turn manure and the methane it creates into electricity. They came back to Oregon and there are now digesters that combine dairies and energy production, which take a problem and turn it into a solution, which is what synergy is all about.

Scientists from Nanyang Technological University have invented a new toilet system that will turn human waste into electricity and fertilizers and also reduce the amount of water needed for flushing by up to 90 per cent compared to current toilet systems. I suggested to Joani we could get one of those systems.

For once, she actually listened to one of my ideas instead of poopooing it. That might be a good idea, she said. You could personally light up our neighborhood.

What Do I Do About Boston?

Two bombs went off during the 2013 Boston Marathon, killing at least three and wounding 140. The explosions were designed to do the most damage possible to ordinary people.

My company used to send me to hire engineers from MIT in Boston. I have a friend Willie who trained for the Boston Marathon. He's at the top of a younger age group and just about to enter an older category. He just missed the cut-off, but he should qualify for the next one. Still I called his wife Monica and asked, Willie wasn't there, was he?

One woman who lost her daughter in that tragedy, made a statement through her tears, this doesn't make any sense.

I remember what I thought and felt when I heard of the bombings in Boston. It made no sense. It made me ill.

It doesn't make any sense. Most systems of right and wrong are rooted in religious beliefs. Both Jews and Christians are commanded by the Bible, thou shalt not kill. Every religion has a similar taboo. The Quran says, "Take not life, which Allah hath made sacred...." Hindus and Buddhists believe all life is sacred.

Most scientific disciplines in the University avoid addressing the problem of evil. That area is reserved for the philosophy or religion departments. There is a relatively new scientific discipline, however, that has taken on the problem of evil, the sociobiologists, and they have waded in with a definition - any action which harms the welfare of the species is evil. The greater the harm to the species, the greater the evil.

The questions raised in Boston that have been left unanswered form a roadblock in the mind. It's hard to get on with the rest of our life in the face of questions like, what was the purpose of those explosions? Who was being attacked? Why choose that venue? That method? When Timothy McVeigh blew up the Alfred P. Murrah Building in Oklahoma City, was that not just a fluke? Are we now like the rest of the world, Pakistan, Iraq, Afghanistan, Indonesia, the London subway system, where explosions are a fact of life, where innocents are killed indiscriminately?

So no matter which religion or scientific discipline we consult, by any definition, what happened in Boston was an act so evil it short-circuits our attempt to understand it. It seems to be an attempt at species suicide. It makes no sense. It makes us ill.

What an event like Boston does that is so disquieting is it brings us face to face with our own mortality. It reacquaints us with the knowledge it could all end in an instant. It could be an explosion like happened in Boston, or it could be an auto accident, or our heart could attack us. We've known it, really, all along, at an intellectual level, but what Boston does is bring it to a visceral level. It brings it to the pit of our stomach. It makes us ill.

It means us, personally. It means that the merry-go-round we're on is not going to stop. It will go on its merry way. It's us. At some point, our ride will end. At some point, at any time, we're going to have to get off.

So what are we to do in the face of that fact?

There is an antidote to Boston. We can stop and look at our friends, our co-workers, our family. We can realize the irritants that seemed so annoying are nothing, really. When they, or we, could disappear in a heartbeat, we could stop and tell them through a few words or small actions, I appreciate you, you have enriched my life, I'm better because I've known you. I'm better because I've known you.

You're Above Average

Are you above average? I'll bet you are, aren't you? All my friends and family are above average. If you don't believe me, ask them. I must be below average because somebody has to be.

If you peruse the major categories of life, all of you fall into the higher-than-average category. Remember the bell curve from statistics? All of you are located on the right-hand side.

I'm a really good driver, I hear all the time. Just the other day I heard someone say it while she was draining the last of her third beer in a pub while I was doing research for this column. She was probably going to call someone to pick her up since she was over the minimum legal alcohol limit and since she was an above average driver. Or maybe she was going to take a cab. That would be hard in our area since there isn't cab service in South County.

I have never heard anyone ever say, my driving? Oh, I'm really below average. Not once. Everyone I have ever heard describe their driving skills, amazingly, is on the right-hand side of the driving bell curve.

The left-hand side? Just me. I hold down the average for everyone else, and I'll tell you, it's pretty lonely over here.

My night vision is not as good as it used to be. I miss turns, drive over curbs, am honked at while I'm backing up, drive too close to the edge or center of the road, scrape the side of our car against shrubs leaving friends' houses, have provided some business to auto body repair shops, and frightened my wife Joani who's hard to scare. She doesn't drive but helps me out when she thinks my driving doesn't come up to average which is pretty much nonstop.

As a columnist? If you read Joel Stein, Dave Barry, Maureen Dowd, Noam Chomsky, or Garrison Keillor, I'm definitely below average, although I think I'm funnier than Chomsky.

Garrison Keillor says all the women are strong, all the men are good looking, and all the children are above average in Lake Woebegone. If you want to insult someone, tell them they're average.

I had a fellow teacher get in big trouble once. Why, Mr. Storey, did I get a C, a student asked him. Because you're average, he said. He tried to explain. A few at the top, a few at the bottom, but most of you are average by definition. You're one of them.

He also got to have a meeting with her parents and a conference with the principal. We have an entire education system based on the concept that every child should be above average.

What other areas of life is everybody above average? Most cooks claim to be better than average cooks. If you ask a kid about their prowess on a video game, all of them claim to be above average. The elderly will be happy to tell you, when comparing their wisdom, their above average but the next generation is way below average.

Another category is friendship. If you have a friend, with, say, bad breath, an above average friend would mention it, right? Wrong. If you want to get moved to the left-hand side of the bell curve, just open your mouth. Your job as an above-average friend is to smile and take a step backwards.

Most men claim to be on the right hand side of the lover bell curve. Now that I think about it, most of those claims were made when they were in their twenties. Still, I suppose their opinions haven't changed. Like I said, it's lonely on the left.

The Butt of the Joke

I write a humor column. Okay, it's been argued both ways, but I insist I do. The challenge to writing humor is somebody has to be the butt. How do you make a joke without hurting someone's feelings? I've already gotten in trouble several times with my editor for insulting half the residents of Tillamook County. If you're the butt, you know how it feels.

You probably have some favorite jokes that target men, women, children, teens, the elderly, ethnic groups, Texans, almost anyone but yourself. That's why humor directed at oneself, self-effacing humor, virtually taking off your face you present to the world so you can be seen, warts and all, is so charming. It shows you're comfortable in your own skin and you don't have to insult anyone else to be funny. You've solved the humor dilemma. You're the butt.

I say all this because I mean no disrespect to Maxwell's Restaurant, a good eating place with friendly service located in Lincoln City. I lost a pool game in league play recently at Maxwell's. It was my son's fault.

Both of my sons are funny. I like to think it's evidence they're actually my sons. I'm envious of my youngest son Josh who can repeat complete comic shticks he's heard once.

Although my older son Patrick who lives in Texas is a religious fundamentalist and as far as I know he's never blown anything up, still, he too has a great sense of humor.

During a weeklong visit each year, there are inevitable slow periods and occasionally Patrick will read ads and make funny comments to entertain us. Something about Maxwell's makes Patrick laugh. Two-for-One Sirloin Steak Special, he'll read aloud. Mmmm, he will say. Hey, if we hurry, we can catch the early bird special at Maxwell's.

Maybe he's a secret vegetarian. It's an unknown fact, but vegetarianism is against the law in Texas. Or maybe it's Maxwell's extensive collection of Betty Boop paraphernalia.

I know how Maxwell's must feel.

I fancy myself a cook. After I had served Patrick a dish I had worked for hours on, crab cakes I'd made from Dungeness crabs I'd caught myself in the ocean in my own dory boat off Pacific City, boiled, cleaned, picked and served with mango salsa, Patrick pushed himself back from the table, patted his stomach, and said, man, was that filling.

A few nights ago I played league pool at Maxwell's. About half way through, I heard an electric hum that I could feel in my heel bones. A voice reverberated throughout the cavernous dance hall over a PA system set on 9. Then the music started. Unable to hear each other, we pool players had to use sign language to indicate which ball was called in which pocket. I made the mistake of thinking of Patrick and couldn't stop laughing.

I lost the game but it was his fault. After all, how could I sink a long shot while laughing at my son's grinning face while I listened to the locals sing rock and roll karaoke at Maxwell's?

Now you can appreciate my skill in writing humor. Even though I wrote this piece, and Maxwell's was the butt, it's Patrick's fault. As for the folks at Maxwell's, even though you probably don't have a Maxwell's joke, I'm sure you have a Texas joke, and since Patrick is in Texas two thousand miles away, why should you care?

As for my other son Josh, I'll get to you later.

Hugging - Can You Dig It?

Perhaps a reaction to all the bad news going round is more hugging.

When I was in school during the stone tablet era, we boys (we never thought of ourselves as men) certainly didn't hug. We didn't shake hands. In fact, we never touched unless it was a fist to the face. Girls didn't hug as often as they do today. Boys and girls didn't hug each other unless they were alone.

Now it is impossible for one group of young people to meet another without everyone hugging everyone else. All the girls hug. Boys and girls hug. Boys have progressed from the fist bump, to the occasional hug. I expect to see more male hugs. I suspect young people get in less trouble because they spend more time hugging each other.

President Obama does the man hug. That's where you shake hands while grabbing each other's hand-shaking shoulder in a sort of half hug. The hands remain clasped at stomach level so that if pulled close, bellies won't touch.

Like push comes to shove, hugging is a progression of the handshake, which came from the wave, the open palm to show we're not carrying a weapon. I find that encouraging. It's hard to be angry when you're holding hands.

My son Josh has shaken some notable hands. Instead of bedtime stories I used to tell him vaudeville routines and so when Sugar Babies, a vaudeville review starring Mickey Rooney and Ann Miller came to town, Joani and I took Josh. Rooney is in front of the stage doing a routine as a handyman banging on things while Ann Miller is trying to sing on stage. They send zingers back and forth.

Since Sugar Babies is a little bawdy, Josh is the only child in the audience. Rooney sees Josh, aisle seat, second row, stands beside him, and holds out his hand. Josh puts his hand in Mickey Rooney's hand. The spotlight widens to encircle Mickey Rooney and our son holding hands as Rooney does his shtick.

Why did he do that? Rooney understood the power of the touch. It's skin to skin. It's personal. It's acceptance. It's a sort of wordless blessing. He was telling Josh, no matter what we say in this skit, I'm taking care of you.

A year later I asked Josh, a third-grader, how was school today? Okay, he said. Anything special happen? He thinks for a minute. Well, he says, President Jimmy Carter visited our school and he shook my hand.

A year later Oregon State Senator Glen Otto was running for reelection. He came to our door and asked for our vote. I invited him inside and Josh came wandering through. Come and meet Senator Otto, I said, who held out his hand, He and Josh shook.

How does it feel, I asked, to shake hands with an Oregon Senator? Well, Josh told Senator Otto, you have to realize I've shaken hands with President Carter and Mickey Rooney.

There is something significant about touching each other. In religious ceremonies, we lay on hands. In the East, a field is believed to be created by the vital energy sent by the practitioners of the Japanese ki, the Chinese chi, and the Indian prana. The king's touch was said to cure disease. Where I came from, deals were sealed with a handshake. We've been blessing with a touch since before Isaac laid hands on Jacob.

The surface of our skin can be warm or cool, dry or moist and carries electric current and our pulse surging just underneath. We communicate more than we think when we shake hands and hug.

Before hiphop and hippies, we fifties' incarnation of the hipster asked, give me some skin, cat. Can you dig it? I knew that you could.

Cool Things to Do with Kids at the Beach

One of the fun nature facts I've run across over the years you can share with your kids is unborn hyenas actually attack and eat each other in utero. *Cool,* your kids will say after you explain to them what in utero means. If you spend time at the beach, whether you live here or rent a getaway cabin for the weekend, inevitably, when your offspring are fighting over the current electronic device of the week, they will remind you of this fact.

What can you do? Here are a couple of activities to keep your kids from performing the hyena trick ex utero. Take them cockle raking. Yes, cockles, like in the old folk song, cockles and mussels alive, alive-o. Cockles are related to clams and they're even more delicious.

You'll need some equipment, a garden rake, the best are the four long-tined ones, a bucket, a $7-shell fish license, kids under 14 free, hip boots or waders for you. Since I've seen kids swimming in the ocean without wetsuits, they can probably get away with wading knee deep. On the plus side, their bodies will use up a lot of energy keeping warm, so they'll most likely take a nap later. Find the tide on your smart phone, the lower the better. The best place is South County at Wayland Island. South from Tillamook, take the Sand Lake Rd. turnoff to Pacific City. About a half-mile before Tierra del Mar, turn at the bridge. Park and hike west to the estuary a couple hundred yards.

The cockles are everywhere and most likely you'll see others raking. My last check on limits is twenty-five per person. I routinely gathered my twenty without moving. Rake, pick them up, put them in your bucket. That's about it. Since they're large meaty bivalves, that should be more than enough for a dinner.

Kids love this. It's like finding ugly Easter eggs. They'll probably be better at it than you. Steam them until they open, clean the little green stomach out, cut in strips, dip in a batter of 1 cup milk, 1 cup flour and 2 egg yolks. Roll in cornmeal or panko. Fry for seconds in hot oil. Better than anything you can buy and you can pontificate about the connection between work and dinner.

If it's raining sideways, make homemade marshmallow. They're delicious, nothing like the white pillows in bags. In a small bowl mix three packets of unflavored gelatin and ½ cup water, set aside. Bring 1 ½ cup sugar ½ cup corn syrup, ½ cup water to a gentle boil in a medium saucepan until a candy thermometer reaches 240 degrees. Be careful. Boiling sugar on the skin is like napalm. Scrape bloomed gelatin into a mixing bowl and turn the mixer on low. Gently pour in the boiling sugar. Slowly raise the speed to high and beat for 15 min. You have marshmallow. If you only have a hand mixer, an adult beats for a few minutes until the mixture begins to turn white. Hand it off to a kid for five minutes. Switch kids every five minutes until 15 min. I rarely ever eat a commercial marshmallow, but I think I could eat the entire batch of this stuff.

Mix ½ cup cornstarch and ½ cup powdered sugar and put in a pan. Scrape the marshmallow into the pan, mash flat, pick up and turn over until all sides are coated. Eating the marshmallow while your doing this is required. Let sit for an hour or so. Cut and eat.

Your kids now have a sugar high which brings us back to the hyena metaphor.

Eight Degrees of Perspiration

The problem with trying to write a humor column about global warming is, it's not very funny.

Oh, sure, I might get a smirk from you when I say, will the last polar bear leaving the Arctic, please turn off the Northern Lights?

But see? Tough.

There's nothing funny about enough CO_2 to make a greenhouse of our planet. Wait a minute, you say. The earth's already a greenhouse, quoting Elton John in Rocket Man, "Mars ain't the kind of place to raise your kids. In fact, it's cold as hell." Mars, space, who can argue with Elton John?

And what's wrong with a longer growing season, I can hear you ask. Maybe I'll finally get my tomatoes to ripen in this soggy county.

Water vapor isn't funny, either. It's being piled on top of carbon dioxide. That's why we have extreme flooding. Trust me, a county with seven major rivers when November comes is no laughing matter.

I've a friend with way too much time on his hands who obsesses on the hockey stick. The hockey stick is a hockey-stick shaped graph for average temperatures for the earth. For most of our existence we were bopping along, singing a song until 1900 when earth's temperature started to rise dramatically due to burning coal and petroleum in the Industrial Revolution. One side says humans are the cause of the hockey stick graph. The other side says there isn't one and we didn't cause it.

Dissolved CO_2 makes the oceans acidic which impedes the formation of shells. I'll grant naked crabs would be pretty funny and a lot easier to eat. If you don't think so, you need to be whacked with a naked crab.

The earth has heated 1.3 degrees since 1900. Predictions project an average rise in temperature of the earth of another six or so degrees by 2100, totaling almost eight degrees warmer. That may not seem like much, but during the last ice age the earth's temperature was only eight degrees cooler and we had mile-thick glaciers over New Jersey. Granted, that would have improved New Jersey, but you get my point.

Emitting greenhouse gasses will become socially unacceptable eventually like smoking in a restaurant. You'll select the raw food entree and complain to the waiter, "Will you please put out that wood-fired grill? I'm trying to eat dinner here without melting Antarctica."

Actually, I wouldn't worry about it. It's probably too late. Carbon dioxide will continue to heat up our atmosphere for hundreds of years. Soon you'll be able to water-ski across the Arctic Ocean.

We're changing the planet. You may have already noticed. Flowers bloom earlier, droughts last longer, like the one last year. Heat waves are hotter, like the one this year. Winters are warmer like the last one. Migratory patterns are changing. Birds arrive to eat larvae, which have already morphed to whatever they were going to be, butterflies or hippies or something, and carpooled to the next music festival.

The ocean has risen eight inches since 1900 and is predicted to rise another three feet by 2100. That won't quite put cities underwater, but storm surges like the one that hit New Orleans and New York will do trillions of dollars of damage. How does the Chicago Yankees sound?

Don't worry your pretty little head about any of this. Let your kids do it. Long before then you'll be busy telling your life story to someone feeding you dinner at four o'clock in the afternoon who doesn't speak English.

Now, that's funny.

In Search of America

A while ago Joani and I went looking for America in a 69 Buick convertible. We took the smallest roads we could find. What if we get lost? Joani asked. We can't get lost. We don't know where we're going.

In Goldendale, WA, we visit the Maryhill Museum, originally built by Sam Hill, as in where-in-the. It is about as ugly a structure as a man can make. He built it for his wife, who took one look at it and moved to Portland. It was instructive. It's what happens when pure logic is used without consulting the heart. It may seem a stretch, but I don't think it is, to connect Sam Hill's house and the killing fields of Cambodia or Mao Tse Tung's Great Leap Forward. All logic, no heart.

In Molalla we met Rita Cooper who invited us to stay for Western Days and Sheep Undressing. Men try to catch a sheep dressed in a bikini, transfer the bikini to themselves and run to the finish line with their sheep in their arms where they're judged in a beauty contest. I thought of the Tillamook Pig 'N Ford races.

In Thermopolis, Wyoming in a barroom where outlaws threw down whiskeys, we met sisters Connie and Belinda who'd taken time away from their business attire to come home to move Daddy's cattle up country. After throwing back a couple ourselves to honor Butch and Sundance who drank there, they invited us to go along. Turns out 'up country' is forty miles and fifteen hours in the saddle. We declined.

There is a cowboy bar and an Indian bar in Interior, SD. The cowboy bar was empty. We tried conversation in the Indian bar, but it was hard to bridge the cultural gap. I asked questions about Custer and The Hole-in-the-Wall Gang. "The

Sioux ran them off," the alpha male tells me, ice in his voice until Joani picks up, holds in her lap and talks to one of their toddlers running around the bar. The gap melts. We're invited to a big powwow in a week.

John and Myrtle sit next to us at The Pole Barn in Mountain View, MO. We asked John, where are the trees? "There used to be three factories around here," John said, "making hardwood floors. Now we have the charcoal cutters. They used to just cut the large trees. Now they cut everything. You have similar problems in Oregon, do you not, no trees for the next generation?"

Max Plinckard in Fordyce, AK, admired the car and said, "God, you're from the Northwest. I wish I were up there now. I owned three motels in Medford, Ashland, and Grants Pass." He has a faraway look in his eyes. "Think of me when you pass the Siskiyous."

Twice we were followed, once by a white guy in Louisiana with a rifle in his gun rack, once by a car full of blacks in Mississippi. They asked if they could help since they suspected we didn't know where we were going. Turns out you can get lost after all. Both times we were told to follow and we were escorted where we wanted to be.

At the Red Rose Tavern and Restaurant in Hayes, LA we meet Red and Delta Giles who after an hour want to adopt us. We could live in the mobile home out back. They have a charity, the Hot Box Brothers and Sisters, who go anywhere they're needed to do charity work by cooking. They went to Lake Percy, Nebraska to help out a widow and cooked 236 gallons of gumbo.

In seven weeks and 8500 miles we never heard a discouraging word except in Nevada stopping at a neon beer sign when Bev Hurrell wouldn't let Joani come in to get a diet soda unless she wanted to go to work.

Work? I thought. I then saw the name of the place, Cotton Tail Ranch.

We found America. It's courteous and helpful and for the most part not on the 6:00 o'clock news.

Smart As Congress

If pressed, maybe you could think of somebody, like maybe your boss, you'd like to push in front of a train. A short time ago, a woman pushed a man to his death in front of a subway train because he was "Muslim or Hindu and 911." The man was neither. And it was the second such incident in a month.

If you've been to Portland recently and tried to find a parking space, you may not think of the Earth, Mars, and Moon as unimaginably large, distant and impervious gods of space. We have left our junk on the moon, are exploring Mars with a robot with a broom that tidies up a bit and even Earth now seems small and fragile.

Singly, we are brilliant. Members of our species have used their brains like magic vehicles to travel out of our solar system, to the furthest reaches of the universe which, they have concluded, is screaming away from us at unimaginable speeds. You may not have known you contributed tax dollars to build a machine that travels back in time to the beginning of the Universe, that can approach the speed of light and create conditions like in the beginning of all things.

We have traveled to the infinitely small spaces between subatomic particles, which somehow become vast in their smallness, mirroring outer space. We have coursed through the veins of the human body, fixed broken brains of the living, operated on babies still inside the pregnant mother, and yet we can do nothing about Donald Trump's hair.

We as a species are not as smart as our smartest. We are as smart as the mob screaming for the death of those who spell God's name differently. We are as smart as those who thought, through some twisted artistic judgment, we could make babies more beautiful than when they were born, think Tillamook Flatheads, by strapping them to boards to flatten their heads, causing a large number to go blind. We are as smart as the Chinese who broke the feet of their six-year-old girls so they could bind them and force four of their toes to touch their heels, leaving only the great toe on which to walk, causing the death of one in ten of them.

Lest you shake your head in smugness at these barbaric practices, it's the same type of twisted judgment that says women are more beautiful when they cram their toes into pointed shoes because it forces their heels high in the air, their breasts forward, their buttocks back and causes foot, leg and back injury to the six out of ten women who wear high heels. Don't you want to be a Kardashian?

We are as smart as a any group who thinks it would be a great idea to get rid of another group they're living with, like Hitler did with the Jews, Hutu/Tutsi did with each other, and our Pilgrims, Davy Crockett and a dozen or more U. S. Presidents did with the American Indian.

I know what you're thinking. Why can't we do the same for Congress, which, in a recent poll is now ranked lower in approval than root canals, schoolyard bullies, and Lindsay Lohan.

It's not brainpower we're lacking. We know how to solve our problems. Stop trying to solve them by killing those we disagree with, even if they are Democrats.

It's not brainpower. It's will power. It's the will power to see the other as ourselves. It's the will power to see differences not as threatening, but as interesting and beautiful, even if she is your mother-in-law.

It's not even will power. It's heart power.

In Defense of Defense

The gun debate rages anew. Because of a personal experience, I've changed my mind.

Seagulls don't like birdseed. Apparently someone forgot to tell all of them because one took over our bird feeder. I tried to shoo it away but it was immune to being shooed. My wife had emptied a beer can. I crumpled it up and threw it at the seagull eating our black oil sunflower seeds. It flapped a couple times, rose a foot in the air, settled back on the bird feeder and resumed eating.

Something inside me snapped. I have never been very territorial, but being unable to protect my property and loved ones from aggressive wildlife caused a change deep inside the cells of ancient tribal mind, a buss switching current from one circuit to another. In a nanosecond, I became a hunter/killer.

I dropped what I was doing, went to the store and bought a BB gun, which I nicknamed Old Blue. It had a list of ten rules sent by Red Ryder, or his agents. I realized I had already broken three of them. It also had instructions that a parent should sign the enclosed permission slip, which I mailed to my father who claimed was further proof he was in the Navy overseas when I was conceived.

I called my neighbor Tom Sloan, a 70-year-old titan of business, told him my situation and asked him if he would help me sight it in my Red Ryder air rifle. He delayed a high-level conference call. We put a cardboard box in his yard and we fired Old Blue across the neighbor's yard and into his yard for the next hour until we were crack shots.

The next morning during my first cup of coffee I swiveled my head to see my bird feeder invaded by a seagull. It had to be the same one. I named it Jonathon Seagull. This was personal.

I grabbed Old Blue, slipped open the deck door and took careful aim. I have to admit, I was a bit shaky.

I fired. There was a loud squawk, a couple of feathers swirled and Jonathon took off in frightened flight.

It is impossible to relate the guttural joy I felt. Instantly the gun lobby's arguments made perfect sense. I realized the 2nd Amendment protected my right to use Old Blue to defend my family.

The next morning I saw a seagull on our birdfeeder. Was it Jonathon, I wondered? It was eating birdseed that rightfully belonged to yellow finches.

Once again with stealth and practiced, battle-hardened calm, I fired again. This seagull squawked and was air born. It landed on the roof in front and eyed me maliciously. I crouched, steadied for a long distance shot and fired. The practice paid off. I hit that seagull and he took flight. I still wondered if that was a different seagull or Jonathon.

The next morning, a seagull fed at our bird feeder. I leveled my one good eye with a steely gaze. Eventually, the seagull looked up and our eyes locked.

The seagull squawked loudly, spread his wings and careened into air without me so much as me firing a shot. It indeed had been Jonathon. By protecting my property with Old Blue, I could now vanquish my foe with a glance.

Now I know the true meaning of an eye for an eye.

When I feel agitated or I'm succumbing to the pressures of being retired, I calm my nerves by patrolling our perimeter, and in my right hand, faithful Old Blue, my right to do so protected by the United States Constitution.

Your Granddaughter's Granddaughter

There are 2 people in the U.S. with the name of Schubert Moore. If your name is Mary Jones, there are 21,019 of you.

Since time began 106 billion people (Don't ask; I have no idea.) have shared the common breathing space on this planet. 99 billion have since passed into oblivion.

Archeologists estimate that nearly 250 thousand years ago, Homo sapiens (modern humans) emerged in Africa, per one theory, or arose simultaneously world wide, according to another. We passed on our history verbally, usually with a beat you could dance to, until cuneiform started recorded history with the invention of the first tablet about 5000 years ago. The software crashed if you dropped it.

I met my great grandfather on my mother's side, in fact, knew him well. He rarely spoke. He could. I heard him on two occasions. Once he said in a clear voice sitting at a dining room table with two dozen relatives eating a Thanksgiving dinner, "I don't like this ice cream."

Conversation froze at his words. "Well, Dad," my grandmother said, "what seems to be the matter with it?" She tasted it and broke into laughter. In the cleanup chaos before dessert was served, someone had scooped for him mashed potatoes.

I do not know the name of the woman who birthed the woman who birthed Mattie Evelena Moore, my grandmother. Even if someone told me what it was, that's all I would know about her.

I would not know if she ever pressed a flower between the pages of a journal so that one day you, my great, great grandson, she might say to me if she could, will know I existed and breathed the same air you're breathing now, that I had a name, and this is what I held dear. This was my greatest accomplishment. This is what I believed. If I had had the right to vote, this is who I would have voted for. I got this scar when I was struck in the face. This is who I flirted with. And this is the flower I pressed for you in my journal now long lost.

It is hard to understand the fact that the granddaughter of my granddaughter, Rowan, will not know that I existed. She will never know I shot a fair game of pool, that I'm a published poet and author, and that I couldn't fix my own car if someone held a gun to my head. She will never know I lived in Tillamook County, my idea of heaven on earth. She will never know I'm not surprised by tragedy but beauty in any form leaves me wet-eyed.

I know what some would say. Oh, don't worry about it. This life is just a preparation for the next one, anyway.

But I think this life is pretty important. The thought that in four generations from now no one will know your name or what you fought for or whom you loved, is the sort of fact that, in this life, anyway, takes the breath. I tried to find out how many names appear in recorded history, Shakespeare, Socrates, Buddha, King George III, but I couldn't. When compared with 106 billion people, though, pretty small. Everyone knows Columbus. No one knows who his cobbler was.

Maybe I got it all wrong. Maybe the internet has made all our words immortal, but I don't think so. The truth is, if it's a needle in a haystack, it's lost.

I'll have to accept the fact my granddaughter's granddaughter will never read these words. That's all right. You have and that will have to be enough.

Bicycles Begin the Long Goodbye

By the time you read this, 3000 bicyclists will have descended on Pacific City along with support crews and extra vehicles, temporarily expanding our population from 500 to 6000.

I heard a lot of complaining from the locals. I'm staying home. I'm watching a movie. But I think they're secretly proud. Who wouldn't want to get out and walk around among the Reach-the-Beachers? What a totally positive event. It's not even a race. You win if you arrive. What a target-rich environment for us people-watchers. And bicyclists have a different frame of mind. Would you prefer 3000 Harley-Davidson riders?

They've forgotten they had their first taste of freedom on a bicycle.

I've never ridden in the Reach-the-Beach bicycle ride, but some years earlier I rode from Salem to Lincoln City with a dozen friends. I remember sharing Hwy 22/18 with logging trucks in a downpour.

Although there have been some developments in bicycle seats, back then they weren't all that comfortable. Let's just say bicycle seats occupy some pretty personal space and soon into the trip I noticed at the first break I wasn't walking my usual walk.

Also, there have been developments in clothing. In the immediate post-Schwinn Speedster era, we typically wore what we gardened in. I've been told one doesn't wear underwear with compression shorts. Let's just say I don't know about you, but I don't want anything compressed, underwear or not.

Even though the organizers try to make this a safe event, every year I see the mixture of bicycles and autos and trucks and trailers on the Reach-the-Beach Route, Hwy 130, The Little River Road, and it makes me shiver. It has no bike lane, a mixture of narrow road, sheer drop-offs, logging trucks, trailers of sand buggies pulled by pickups fueled by more than gas, and one-lane bridges. Sure enough, last year one rider was killed.

I sound like I got old, right? Well, that's not it. I'm still crazy after all these years. Insane. Certifiable. I'm 71 and I went on my first solo Harley ride less than a year ago. I've skied twenty-six miles across the McKenzie Pass in the middle of winter in a whiteout. I fell in a crevasse in Hell's Kitchen climbing Mount Hood solo with one crampon. Portland has the reputation of being the most bike-friendly city in the U.S. I thought it would be cool to commute by bicycle six miles to work from Northeast to Southeast. After being struck twice in three months, I hung it up.

No gift to a child represents a maturity dividing line more than a bicycle. I remember my first, a heavy one-speed I used like a demolition derby racer playing tin can polo on our dead-end street. Just before a bicycle, children are in that special time of cuteness that parents remember so poignantly it makes our heart hurt, past toddler but not yet, what, a fledgling? They haven't left the nest, even for a look around.

After a bike they're a kid.

The gift of a bike is the beginning of the long goodbye. On a bike they can be out of your sight before you can turn around. Before bikes, you have the illusion of control, of creating a bubble of protection so nothing bad will ever happen. Every boo-boo can be kissed away.

If you haven't already, one day you will run along beside them, your hand on the seat, keeping them balanced, until you feel them pulling away under their own power.

You take a deep breath and let them go.

Mr. News Guy Explains Conspiracy Theories

It's time once again for Mr. News Guy to explain the puzzling behavior of, well, us.

At a recent meeting we were told whether we like it or not, we would be getting electricity-generating devices out in the ocean. There is the chance we would be able to see these structures, which means it would affect our ocean view, and if we could ignore them during the day, to make sure we didn't miss them at night, they would be lighted.

No one likes to be told they have no say in the matter. It sprouts conspiracy theories. Mr. News Guy is from the buckle of the Bible belt. He was raised on conspiracy theories, which is the belief in a complicated plot by a secret group.

Mr. News Guy has been warned there was a conspiracy to poison him by dumping fluoride in his drinking water, there is a zoo of aliens in Area 51 in Nevada, and the Communists, Jews and Masons had it in for him using Edward R. Murrow, the International Banking System and black helicopters owned by the New World Order. He was informed we attacked ourselves on 9/11 and we landed on the moon in a studio set in California. Mr. News Guy points out there are thousands of conspiracy theories, one for every hard-to-believe, difficult-to-understand event.

We believe in the cause and effect rule of thumb, that is, big results should have big causes. It makes more sense to believe 9/11 was a complicated conspiracy to get us into war than it is to believe a few guys with box cutters on a Tuesday could bring down the World Trade Center.

If you're on the lookout for conspiracy theories, they're always trying to take over the world. Mr. News Guy believes anyone who wants to take over the world deserves it.

Some prefer to believe global warming is a conspiracy, because if it isn't, it means we have to change the way we live.

Who are these conspirators, we demand, slamming our fist down on whatever hard surface is handy, who are going to ruin our ocean view?

Mr. News Guy hates to remind us, but we have asked every candidate for President from Johnson to Obama to reduce buying energy in the form of sweet crude from the Middle East. Drill, baby, drill became our motto.

Also, at our request the Federal Government supported the increase in gas mileage, fracking for gas and oil here at home, clean coal, and hydro. They funded the search for alternatives, green energy in the form of solar panels, algae farms, and wind and wave electricity generation. We demanded of our candidates, do something to make us energy secure. When they reassured us that they would, we voted for them.

Well, they listened to us. We're going to get what we asked for. The Federal Government has put a plan together to create electricity from the ocean like we citizens demanded. We heard you, the Federal Government responded. If you run into problems doing it yourself, we'll help out by doing it for you.

Yes, but we didn't mean *here!*

Mr. News Guy thinks he found the secret group plotting the conspiracy.

He thinks the secret group is us.

Reality or Illusion – Take Your Pick

Poet T. S. Eliot said between the dream and the reality falls the shadow. We strive to stay in touch with reality, but we can do quite well without it much of the time. However, we couldn't get through the day without a couple of juicy illusions.

I depend on an illusion. Recently I got an ocular prosthetic or glass eye. The eyes hold tremendous power. Without it, when people are trying to speak to me, they can't keep from staring. They lose their train of thought. With the illusion of two normal healthy eyes, they're free to continue to remember what they were trying to say.

But Schubert, I can hear you thinking, I don't depend on illusions to get through the day.

Wrong. Clothes are illusions. Shoulder pads in men's suits to make them look bigger and stronger, and for women when they were in fashion in the 1940's and 80's to make them look, well, more like men who held most of the power back then. Clothes make your waist slim, your shoulders broad, your chest big and socks the same color of the slacks to extend the leg, your legs longer. Heels and lifts make you taller. Black and vertical stripes slim. I mentioned this to my mother once. She responded, that's why, I suppose you're inferring, I look like I've done my clothes shopping at Portland Tent and Awning?

Ever see a woman go to work without makeup? Blush to give the illusion of vibrant health. Sarah Palin knew. Lipstick. Jewelry to create the illusion of wealth. Men in prison stuff their shirts with toilet paper to protect themselves by making them look more muscular. Do I really need to explain padded bras?

A couple we know met in a nudist resort. I think the real reason that makes most minds' brainscan go blank at this thought doesn't have much to do with modesty. The thought that everyone would see our weak-shouldered, short-legged, small-chested, big-waisted, pale, poor, chubby little body makes our system crash. We'd be stripped of not just clothes, but our illusions.

Ever had cosmetic dental work done, padded a resume, embellished the truth at a party? How about those brag and gag letters sent out during the holidays? Your child has developed a cure for cancer? Really?

We can get our heads around wigs, maybe even hair plugs, possibly even toupees, but the comb over? Spray-on hair? Really? Even the current popularity of the expression Really? challenges the illusion.

The reason people don't want their picture taken is it's easy to see through the illusion.

There's one place though where illusion creates reality. A research study in 2004 by University College London found that feelings of love suppressed critical thought, meaning, love is blind. When I look at my wife, I can't see her. Even with one good eye, I don't see a graying, sixty-nine-year-old woman in a wheelchair. I see the full-lipped, full hipped, mahogany-haired beauty I fell in love with forty-two years ago. I'll keep that illusion, thank you.

Who knows what she sees?

Feigning Interest Can Save Your Marriage

Recently a radio program featured an interview with Kristin and her husband Dave who has Asperger's Syndrome, a form of autism, or as Kristin calls him, an aspie. Aspies are characterized by emotional distance, missing social cues, clumsiness, limited empathy, and taking only what they need out of the dryer. I know, your opinion is every man is an aspie.

A successful aspie technique is to imitate normal people. One thing aspies can do is learn how to listen. It's called feigning interest, or pretending to care. Once my wife Joani came home complaining about personality conflicts in a group she was in. Since I wasn't really interested, when I realized she had noticed my eyes had glazed over I asked, can I do something?

No, Joani said. I don't want you to do anything. I want you to be quiet, listen to me, and at the end say, gosh, that's got to be rough for you.

Eager to help, I said, I could do that. I was already good at feigning interest. Making eye-contact while blinking occasionally and nodding, wondering what my next column would be about, let me get a lot done. When she stopped talking, I waited two heartbeats and then repeated the phrase she told me to say, gosh, that's got to be rough for you.

Feigning interest I found was fairly common. I caught Joani feigning interest while I was describing some problem launching the dory through the surf. Gosh, that sounds interesting, she repeated mechanically while she figured out which stamp went where in her album. Joani will watch Three Stooges comedies but isn't interested no matter how many eye pokes or fart jokes are in it. It's a puzzle.

Kristin said, even though Dave is faking the empathy, the fact that he goes through the motions shows he cares. Funny, but that's enough, she said.

Kristin and Dave have a website you can go to, to force your husband to take the aspie test, (males are four times more likely to be an aspie) to determine if he's an aspie or just a typical husband - rdos.net/eng/Aspie-quiz.php.

Sample questions with my comments:

Do you get frustrated if you can't sit on your favorite seat? – You mean no matter if I always sit there and everybody knows it?

Do you have one special talent that you have emphasized and worked on? – No one seems to know how difficult it is to create body music.

Have you been accused of staring? – I was not staring and it was a beauty pageant.

Dave found he could mimic others and be taken for normal by using behaviors he noticed others used, like lowering his voice and slowing down his delivery to mimic sincerity.

I learned a lot from this story and taking the quiz. For instance, Joani came in upset. She said, I'm tired of how dirty this floor is. I feel like I have to do everything myself!

Using what I'd learned, I slowed my delivery, lowered my voice and said, gosh, that's got to be rough for you.

Pursuit of Happiness

When we declared independence from Great Britain, we had to take a number. Actually America was first in line followed by Barbuda, Bahamas, Bahrain, Barbados, Belize, Botswana, Burma, and that's just the B's. Good thing they went in alphabetical order or we'd still be wearing bowlers. Britain was into collecting countries like chess sets.

Independence is in. Everybody wants to be independent, even your kids. Great, you'd like to reply. Go. Be free. Send me an email when you form a constitution and find work.

In the most famous sentence in the English language, Thomas Jefferson wrote, we hold these truths to be self-evident, that all men are created equal, that they are endowed by their Creator with certain unalienable Rights, that among these are Life, Liberty and the Pursuit of Happiness.

Everyone argues almost every word of that sentence. SELF-EVIDENT has generated a lot of discussion. All men are created equal spawned the Civil War and Women's Suffrage. Believers, agnostics and atheists are still arguing about a CREATOR. We keep adding to UNALIENABLE RIGHTS. Did Tommy Jefferson really mean that one of your rights is to paint an American flag on your bums in pink and dance down the street?

LIFE is both used in the abortion controversy and the right to protect yourself by buying a 3.5 rocket launcher, on sale at Walmart this weekend. LIBERTY engendered such controversy it created its own political party.

PURSUIT OF HAPPINESS stops us in our virtual tracks. What the heck is that? I can hear the scratching of heads all over this country.

I have the right to be happy? No, that's not what it said. You have the right to pursue happiness. Oh, I get it, you light up. I can accomplish that by a divorce, retroactive abortions, and a time machine to go back and actually listen in class.

The original wording was life, liberty and property, which, by the way, yours needs mowing. So is happiness things we own? A recent self-reporting poll indicated people who make over $75K are happier than those who don't.

One respondent said happy people are easier to govern. Can we accomplish that with heavy sedation? I see a lot of self-sedation around July 4th. They seem pretty happy.

It's significant that Jefferson, known as a great writer, chose that phrase and it made it through several proofreaders known for high standards, Franklin, Hamilton and the like.

Happiness is a funny word for such a serious document, literally a declaration of war, written by such serious men. And in that lies genius.

The people who founded this country were rejects. We were mold breakers. We couldn't get along in Europe. Our plays-well-with-others box wasn't marked. If you couldn't figure out what to do with serial lawbreakers in Great Britain, you either hanged them or sent them here.

The wig-wearing aristocrats in Europe would never have used a silly word like happiness in a document like The Declaration of Independence. We're going to risk life, limb, treasure and family because we're not happy enough? Outrageous.

Only Americans would do such a thing and this is the day we celebrate it.

What does it mean? You're on your own. Nobody can tell you what to think, anyway. You're too independent.

What Are We Called?

Intrepid Headlight Herald reporter Joe Wrabek in an article about preparedness presented a list of items necessary for survival in case of emergency. First on the list were shoes. Cut feet, Wrabek informed, are the most frequent injury in an emergency. Makes sense. As I went through the rest of his list, I was stopped at crowbar.

I lay there in the dark in bed worrying about emergencies with my shoes close at hand but no crowbar. I imagined how I might use a crowbar. Oddly, none of the images of me using a crowbar in an emergency made me feel safer.

The other items on my side of the bed danced through my head, a kind of animated object musical review. I smiled at Miss Ibuprophen. She smiled back. I was in love with Miss Ibuprophen. I reached out in the dark to make sure she was still there along with other items - tissues, clock, water, etc. Wasn't Mr. Gun supposed to be there somewhere? Maybe Joani moved him.

I felt a sense of panic in the dark. If a huge earthquake caused Tillamook County to separate from the valley and fall into the ocean, we'd be in deep trouble because we had no nickname for our decade.

Other decades had nicknames. The 1890's were called the Gay Nineties when everyone waltzed. The 1920's were called the Roaring Twenties and everyone did the Charleston. The Thirties and Forties, with the Depression, and WWII the nation did the Swing and the Jitterbug, while locally we danced The Tillamook Burn, until the Fifties and that famous plane ride when the music stopped.

In 1962 we experienced two personal emergencies in Oregon. It was hard to tell which did more damage that decade, The Columbus Day Storm or bell-bottoms. There weren't much drugs, sex and rock and roll in the Sixties, which were really the Fifties when everyone slept in twin beds on TV and did The Twist. The Sixties really didn't happen until the Seventies caused by The Funky Chicken.

What's confusing when trying to label time periods is the switch from decades to generations, like Generation X, the generation after the World War II baby boom, known as Boomers which experienced the assassination of John F. Kennedy, the environmental movement, Watergate, Chernobyl, and Black Monday which caused the Berlin Wall to fall down.

I wondered what Generation Y, born somewhere from the '80's to the 2000's, also known as the Millennials, would do in case of an emergency. According to researchers, these trophy kids would alternatingly blame and beg for help from their helicopter parents hovering over them.

9/11 took place in the decade from 2000 to 2010. Another big tragedy was we never came up with a nickname for that decade, either. Oughties, was suggested, you know, like ought six for 2006, but that's confusing because that's what they used for 1906. Another suggestion was the Naughties, like using naught for zero. If you've seen any of the images on your favorite internet appliance, you probably agree the last decade was naughty.

I had another emergency panic attack in the dark. What were we going to call 2011-2019? The teens? If your teens were anything like mine, double entendre intended, I certainly didn't want a decade named after them. Once was enough.

You Need A Nap

A friend called. You sound like you were napping, he said, using the same tone of voice if he were inferring I was of low moral fiber or meth addicted

It's Saturday afternoon. You've mown the lawn, you've had lunch and a beer, and what do you do? Do you announce to your family you're going to take a nap? That would be tantamount to declaring you're going to sun bathe in the nude on the front sidewalk. No, you get a magazine and pretend to read it until your head tilts forward and you drool on the pages.

You, who would always tell the truth no matter what, except about that time in Las Vegas, will lie in a heartbeat without thought if someone awakens you so that your voice sounds like an Egyptian mummy, preferring to admit that you have been dead for three thousand years rather than admit you were taking a nap.

My father never took a nap in his life. He might have been in full Laz-E-Boy recline mode, his mouth open, vibrating the lamp off the end table, but when my mother brought him back to consciousness, he would say, I was just resting my eyes.

I think it's significant the countries with the highest suicide rate, the Japanese, Swedish and Americans, don't take naps, and those cultures with lower rates we dream of going to on vacation, Southern Europe, Antigua, The Bahamas, and other countries with umbrellas in their cocktails, nap daily.

Some of us have to have a nap. Take for instance my lovely wife Joani. Without a nap she might find herself with her frowny face on. Her sister said without a nap her head spins around on her neck like Linda Blair in The Exorcist.

That's silly. I've never seen her head spin around. I have, though, seen her eyes glitter, her teeth bare and heard her, in a guttural voice, speak ancient Sumerian. I just smile, avoid her gnashing teeth, give her a kiss, and come back when she awakens when I find a smiling Disney heroine singing a happy song accompanied by animated blue birds circling her head chirping sweetly in harmony.

I think we'd all be better off taking a daily nap. If you check out the people in the news, you can tell who's napping. I'm sure Michelle makes Barack get some rest every day. Most of the time he's smiling and joking around. He looks well rested. If he puts up any resistance, Michelle just has to mention two words – first debate.

I'll tell you who needs a daily nap, along with a spanking, the President of North Korea, Kim Jong-un. Maybe Dennis Rodman, who I'm sure takes a daily nap along with several self-medications, could get the frighteningly jittery ruler to sleep some in the afternoon between attacks on South Korea. I'm sure threatening half the world must be tiring.

I think a lot of people would benefit from a short nap. I certainly do. A few prone minutes improve my performance considerably doing odd jobs around the house. The last time I gave our car a tune up I worked all day without breaking for a nap. I had to call a tow truck.

I think you can tell just by behavior who's had a nap. I'm sure Lindsay Lohan hasn't had a nap for years. Comedian Jerry Seinfeld must have taken lots of naps. Maybe Eric Snowden should have taken a nap before selecting a country to run to. If Rush Limbaugh ever took a nap, he'd lose his show.

Who else needs a nap? You don't need me to tell you. Congress.

Got the Time?

Time keeps on in slippin', slippin', slippin' into the future. If you got the money, honey, I got the time. What time is it, Yogi Berra was asked. He said, you mean right now? What time is it, my wife Joani asked. What time do you have? She told me. You're five minutes slow. Okay, she replied, began to set her watch, stopped, thought, and said, why is it always my watch that's wrong?

Time, and apparently everything else in the Universe, Einstein said, is a relative relationship, along with your in-law's three hungry teenagers who come to visit unannounced each summer when time slows to infinity.

Do you have the correct time? You might insist you do if you have one of those watches that gets reset from a signal from Washington D. C. based on the vibration of a Cesium atom. That atom has little to do with time.

Researchers questioned elderly who regularly and consistently estimated a time period twenty percent shorter than teens. Who's right? It depends. How much time do you have left, seems to be the conclusion. The less you have the faster it goes. Remember when you were ten or so and weren't allowed to drive, take drugs or gawk at R-rated videos? An afternoon lasted forever, especially when you grew tired of torturing your sibling.

If you don't think time moves at different rates, how long does a summer day last when the sun pours down like honey on buttered toast compared with this coming December 21st when 38° rain will be blowing sideways in that hour of daylight you get to watch it. Why does it take twice as long to get some place unfamiliar as it does to get back?

Eternity isn't something that just happens at the end of your life. Eternity happens all the time. You remember the first time forever took place. It was the first time you had been thinking about confessing your love. What will happen to you if it isn't returned? How will you go on living? It wasn't that you had a lot riding on what you were about to say or anything, just your very existence. You don't know where you got the courage to say what you were feeling. And then from the last word out of your mouth until you heard the response, time stopped. An eternity passed.

Or you're holding your six-months-old child who's been changed, fed, and is sleeping in your arms. Or you've hiked to the top of Eagle Cap in the Wallowa Mountains and a chipmunk has climbed into your lap and is eating your hiking food. Or you're with friends who are trying to find words to describe the sun disappearing into our Pacific pulling a mountain range of pink clouds with it to the horizon, and failing, say nothing at all. You can live an eternity in silence like that.

Those moments are ecstasy and ecstasy is timeless.

Those of us who choose to live at the edge of the earth, although we may seldom put it in words, do so because we can stop time here. We can look up at the stars at night back through the eons to the birth of our Universe when time began. The next morning, we can contemplate the sea swaying, regular as clockwork for all time. The star full night and the endless sea, silence our internal clock. We exist in a sort of grace period, a time without time. We transcend ourselves. It's why we come.

Seeing through heaven and sitting on the sand scanning the sea, stop that swinging pendulum, even though the gulls come in on wings like scythes and shriek their warning – Hour! Hour! Hour! Hour!

Sorry, we're out of time.

Which Are Better – Cats or Grandmothers?

If you're a teen, I'll bet you've been asking yourself, how do your computer skills stack up against your cat? If someone used computer skills and your grandmother in the same sentence, you would roll your eyes.

Cats have recently dominated YouTube. Even the simplest video of a cat using a tablet gathers millions of viewers, whereas no one would be interested in a touch-screen confusing your grandmother.

According to the Nielsen Group, research and training consultants, cats require continual animation, sounds, and a large tap zone. Grandmothers require no tap zone at all since they're afraid to touch the screen. To overcome this barrier, grandmothers can be enticed into interactivity. All you need is Alan Alda from MASH or Dancing With the Stars, or even better, Alan Alda Dancing With the Stars.

One app designer asked, how can I improve our apps for cats and at the same time, cut down on the number of emails from my grandmother? With their lack of opposable thumbs and ever-shifting focus, cats are certainly a challenging target audience.

The Nielsen Group recruited as test participants, average age, 24 months, 16 cats, 4 Persians, 5 Siamese, 3 Russians, 4 British shorthairs, and three blue-haired grandmothers, average age, 912 months. Of the 16 cats, 4 were declawed. Two of the grandmothers recently had their nails done.

All of the cats were allowed outside daily, as were the grandmothers. All of the test users were experienced with traditional cat toys, including balls, milk-jug rings, and cat apps. The grandmothers were app ignorant but were skilled in ordering crystal angels from the Home Shopping Network.

The Nielsen Group tested a total of 28 apps and 12 websites. The most common usability problem was the tap target size on most interfaces. All of the adult cats were clearly frustrated—even hissing—after accidentally closing the apps they were using. The grandmothers didn't hiss, assuming it was their fault and so sent out a barrage of emails to their grandchildren, apologizing.

Conclusions – A sensory-activated "pause mode" is highly suggested, as nearly half the cats randomly stopped what they were doing to lie down on their devices and stretch, nap, or self-groom for extended periods before resuming their tasks.

Grandmothers needed break time to take pies out of the oven.

You may be thinking you prefer your cat over your grandmother due to your grandmother's poor performance on the quiz, but a representative of the Nielsen Group pointed out conclusions which you might, as an inexperienced teen, have missed. It is a violation of the cat code of ethics to remember your birthday, to purchase for you gift certificates to Amazon, or often, to even acknowledge your existence.

Grandmothers, on the other hand, will sit for hours listening to you whine about how unfairly you are treated by her son/daughter, cluck her tongue, nod her head, and give you a seemingly inexhaustible supply of chocolate chip cookies. They are seemingly inexhaustible because they are in fact, inexhaustible. If she ran out of raw materials like chocolate chips, she would make a trip to the store for you.

Another advantage of grandmothers over cats, is her love for you is also inexhaustible, which, according to the Nielsen Group, can never be said for a cat.

Dogs, on the other hand...

Dying in Oregon

My family loves me, I think. I'm in pretty good health, and I have enough to keep me from considering Poptarts an entree. All in all, life's not bad, except for one thing – unasked for advice. Aren't you amazed by the number of people, maybe a neighbor, who can take time away from the Kardashians to tell you how to live and what to think?

When my neighbors and their neighbors feel really strongly about advice, it's called a taboo. If I break a taboo, I could be shunned, jailed, or stoned to death, strictly for my own good. Oedipus found he needed to stick a knife in his eyes because he had broken a taboo. He married Jocasta, his mother, even though he didn't know it and she was a pretty hot babe who could have been a Kardashian if only she'd been born a couple of millennia later.

My wife Joani and I were curious about one taboo. We ordered from Netflix a recent documentary about doctor-assisted suicide, *How to Die in Oregon,* made legal in 1994 and in Washington in 2008. Maybe it's the rainfall.

More than 500 Oregonians have bought that last prescription to help them, in Jim Morrison's words, break on through to the other side. It's usually 100 capsules of Seconal, $150, covered by most medical plans. I wonder what tactics they can resort to if you don't pay.

The capsules are taken apart and the powder mixed with six ounces of room temperature water. A shot of Grey Goose is optional. If you have any last words, best keep it short. It takes only 90 seconds before you stop worrying about the Kardashians. Roger Sagner was the 343rd person to end his life in this manner. He downed the cocktail and said in the minute he had left, "I'd like to thank the wisdom of the voters of the

State of Oregon for allowing me of my own volition to solve my own problems. Tell the next person it tastes woody but it was easy."

Sue Porter is a volunteer for a group called Compassion and Choices. She assists the majority of those who use the law. She says they have to sign a paper that says they request a prescription to end life and they are of sound mind, which I guess eliminates me. It has to be witnessed by two others. Sue asks two questions. Would you like to change your mind? If you drink this, do you understand what it will do?

Gordon Green was having one small heart attack after another. He said his father spent his last twelve years stroke-paralyzed. Gordon said he didn't want to go that way. "If I don't go in my sleep, I'll wash the prescription down with a good, cold beer." When he picked up the prescription, the pharmacist said, "Have a nice day!"

Most of the film followed the last nine months of Cody Curtis, 56, a wife, mother, hiker, and gardener. A year earlier her cancer-ravaged liver stopped working and she ballooned to twice her size. Bedridden and incontinent, her blocked liver forced bile to ooze through the pores of her skin. Extensive chemo gave back her health, but terminal cancer returned. Referring to what she had gone through, she raised her model's high cheekbones and said, "Never, ever again."

If my neighbors meet me in town and want to tell me how wrong I was to explore this issue, I'll suggest they save it for the Kardashians, who've, I suspect, broken enough taboos to keep them occupied through the next TV season.

Mr. News Guy Explains The Nuclear Option

It's time once again for Mr. News Guy to explain confusing developments in the news. Let me just say one word – Congress. Now that I've lost half my audience, the Senate is the part of the Congress with an exclusive zip code. They run for office every six years instead of members of the House of Representatives who run for office every hour and a half. Also, they have better furniture.

In the few nanoseconds when you're flipping channels, your eyes might have stayed on the news long enough for you to realize our Congress isn't working. They're like rival gang members fighting for territory, only instead of Uzis, they're using nuclear weapons.

The nuclear option has something to do with the filibuster, which sounds like something a pirate would say, referring to a gun similar to a blunderbuss. Arrr, give us ye court appointments or we will give ye both barrels of our filibusters, ye scurvy dogs! Ye think I be jesting, ye scurvy reader, well the word root of filibuster means pirate. Never cross swords with a one-eyed columnist.

The purpose of a filibuster is to prevent a vote. Now you might think this is odd since in your imperfect understanding of legislative affairs you foolishly think the purpose of your Senator is to go to Washington to vote on stuff. Wrong. The purpose of a Senator is to go to Washington and NOT vote on stuff. If you vote on things then you have a record and your opponent can use your record against you when they run for your seat in the Senate so they can go to Washington and not vote on stuff.

If you remember that famous documentary starring Jimmy Stewart, Mr. Smith Goes to Washington, a filibuster means you have to stand and speak for hours to delay a vote. Senators found it took a lot of energy and thought to speak for hours unless running for office, so they found they didn't actually have to filibuster. They could just threaten a filibuster and the other side caved. It is the Senate's main contribution.

It was like hiring the Swiss in 16th Century Europe. The Swiss were neutral for a reason. You could hire their army and it was a kick-butt army. If you wanted to go to war against another European country, you didn't actually have to go to war. You hired the Swiss and then you sent a message to the country you planned to attack that you'd hired the Swiss with their multiuse knives and your opponent said, darn! They've hired the Swiss. We concede. Most of this is the truth.

The leader of the Senate Harry Reid recently used the same technique. He threatened to do away with the filibuster. Oh, no! the Senate opposition Munchen-screamed as one, clasping the sides of their heads with the palms of their hands. Do you mean any one of our hundred Senators couldn't stop legislation or delay a vote on a nomination just to drive our rival gang members crazy? We'd actually have to operate like a democracy? Do you mean we'd actually have to vote on something? Yes, the leader of the Senate Harry Reid said, fake-washing his hands while cackling evilly.

Well, they compromised. The Senate actually approved some nominations, one that had been held up for so long reporters had to remind the nominee what office he'd been nominated for.

I know, I know, you've heard of a fantasy Congress in a galaxy far away actually comprising, but this happened here on earth. Of course none of those Senators will be reelected because they compromised which is the latest curse word in politics. Still, it's one of the signs of end times, when lions lie down with lambs and the Senate actually does something.

Lots of luck with the House of Representatives.

You're Too Perfect

I know, I know, perfect is an absolute, like circle, unique, and straight. You can't be very unique. You're either unique or you're not, and quite frankly, I'm a lot more unique than you are.

God must be a perfectionist. You got your purple mountain's majesty. You got your amber waves of grain. You got your Grand Canyon, your Mt. Hood and your Pacific Ocean, the last one in our back yard. I'm not sure how you could improve Mt. Everest, the Gobi Desert or the Amazon Rain Forest. We have chemical scientists inventing stronger and stronger new products and the strongest material on earth is still, pound for pound, a spider's web.

Today is our anniversary. I married a perfectionist. She is meticulous and willing to spend however much time I have to do the job right. In our early years I've thrown up my hands symbolizing I was a gallon of patience low, but she never changed, saying all right, Dear, I'm just about through which I rightly interpreted meant just another eon or two. You're sure it's a health issue if the tops of the cabinets aren't painted?

If God had a wife, I would sympathize with Her, which is stronger than empathize, when She threw up her hands and asked Him, do You know how long You have spent on the Creation? Do You? Six days? Does fourteen billion years ring a bell? And counting!

There are some definite downsides to being a perfectionist, other than worrying whether or not anal-retentive is hyphenated. I tried to explain to a father estranged from his daughter that, when she wrote a letter of reconciliation, he shouldn't correct her spelling. Making sure every single sock has a mate sucks the sweetness out of doing the laundry. Who cares if yellow isn't in the funereal pallet.

Another difference between perfectionists and humans is perfectionists never use the word perfect, whereas the rest of us, me for example, use the word perfect all the time. For instance, if I run out of paint and finish with something we had left over from the last remodel and it looks pretty close with the lights off, perfect, I say, if my wife hasn't seen it.

I have some advice for you perfectionists. You can be so demanding, no one can please you. Everyone goes home unhappy. My advice? The secret to happiness? Lower your standards.

When my mother took six weeks in ICU to die, the team of doctors, each representing an organ of specialty, claimed their particular organ, the liver, for instance was doing great, no one had the big picture. Maybe a few of the organs could have performed a little below perfection and the patient as a whole might have lived for a while longer. I'm just saying.

There are some times when you want a perfectionist. When your mechanic is inside your car's internal combustion engine is a good time to be a perfectionist. Or your newborn has to have heart surgery. Or your accountant is looking for a way to keep the IRS from putting you in jail for claiming your weeklong trip to the Ashland Shakespeare Festival as a job-related deduction because you used the word hamlet in a column.

There is one other time when I recommend being a perfectionist. It has to do with directions. If you're running late, trying to be on time for the reservations to celebrate your anniversary, and you've been with your significant other for some time, and you want to keep what little romance you might still have left, and for whatever reason you have to share a bathroom, and it has a really big mirror in it, and you've just come out of the shower, you might want to double-check which direction you're facing when you dry your ankles.

Don't That Sea Look Wide and Deep

Pam's life might as well have been a Greek drama.

I launched my dory into a flat ocean. The wave came out of nowhere, defying logic, growing like a nightmare.

If I did nothing it would break over the boat, a catastrophe. I put the motor in gear and charged. When I got to the crest, I pulled the throttle back, hoping to slide down the back side. Too late. It had broken under us, leaving us high in the air. We didn't know then, but the fall broke Pam's foot in five places. It was beginning to swell. Pam told Bill to get a bucket of seawater. She stuck her foot in it. She said, let's fish.

Pam died recently. That wave was nothing new. One after another hit her all her life. She was used to them, but when I tell you, you'll want to judge her. You'll frown with disapproval.

In all cultures, it's the strictest taboo. It's unforgiveable. Sophocles wrote Greek dramas based on lesser taboos.

She had five children. She left four of them with an alcoholic husband and took the baby.

She told me if she had stayed she would have died.

Men do it all the time, leave their children. I did. I wasn't ostracized the way we do women. I can think of few taboos as costly. Pam had to pay and pay.

Good, I can hear you whisper.

The first wave to hit Pam was the mother who rejected her, but not her two younger sisters who sat in front of the Christmas tree opening a pile of presents. There is no need for you to come down, her mother told her. Santa didn't bring you anything.

The second wave was when her church, which blamed her for her first husband's homosexuality, rejected and shunned her.

The third wave was her second husband busy drinking himself to death.

But a decision like she made comes with a cost. And how can you live without your family? There was a lot of family repairing to be done. As you might suppose, her children took exception to being abandoned.

Maybe, Pam thought, if I give enough, they'll forgive me. She took in one daughter with MS and was both a grandmother and mother to her children. She provided a house for one, a mobile home for another. She gave money and help to one who couldn't manage to stay out of prison, which probably didn't do anything for Pam's feelings of guilt.

She tried to get on with the rest of her life. She met Bill in the Road Kill Café out West somewhere. If it had been the plot in a romantic comedy it would have been called a cute meet. Instant love. They worried it might not be real. They devised a test. If we still feel the same in the morning, we'll meet at the intersection of two local highways. There they were.

She reached out to all her family, and before she died, she'd just about done it, too. They had forgiven her, as much as you can forgive something like that.

Why didn't she take all the children? Why didn't she kick out her alcoholic husband?

You can't do it, judge her, unless the alcoholic was your husband, her life your life. You can't judge her because your instruction book for living tells you, judge not.

The following year, she came to me and looked into my face with those liquid brown eyes of hers, standing close, as was her way, the way most abused stand close, hoping for approval, and said, I have no right to ask. I'll understand if you say no, but would you take me out in the dory again?

We have a word to describe someone who will not be defeated no matter how the gods conspire. It's a Greek word.

In Defense of Defense

The gun debate rages on. I used to be one of those namby-pamby antigun effete liberals, but because of a what happened, I've changed my mind.

Seagulls don't like birdseed. Apparently someone forgot to tell all of them because one took over our bird feeder. I tried to shoo it away but it was immune to shooing. My wife had emptied a beer can, so I crumpled it up and threw it at the seagull eating our black oil sunflower seeds. It flapped a couple times, rose a foot in the air, settled back on the bird feeder and resumed eating.

Something inside me snapped. I have never been very territorial, but being unable to protect my property and loved ones from aggressive birdlife, caused a change deep inside my cells of ancient tribal mind that switched current from one buss to another. In a nanosecond, I became a hunter/killer.

I dropped what I was doing, went to the store and bought a BB gun, which I nicknamed Old Blue. It had a list of ten rules sent by Red Ryder, or his agents. I realized I had already broken three of them. It also had instructions that a parent should sign the enclosed permission slip, which I mailed to my father who claimed was further proof he was in the Navy overseas when I was conceived.

I called my neighbor Tom Sloan, a 70-year-old titan of business, told him my situation and asked him if he would help me sight it in my Red Ryder air rifle. He delayed a high-level conference call. We put a cardboard box in his yard and we fired Old Blue across the neighbor's yard and into his yard for the next hour until we were crack shots.

The next morning during my first cup of coffee I swiveled my head to see my bird feeder invaded by a seagull. It had to be the same one. I named it Jonathon Seagull. This was personal. I grabbed Old Blue, slipped open the deck door and took careful aim. I have to admit, I was a bit shaky.

I fired. There was a loud squawk, a couple of feathers swirled and Jonathon took off in frightened flight.

It is impossible to relate the guttural joy I felt. Instantly the gun lobby's arguments made perfect sense. I realized the 2nd Amendment protected my right to use Old Blue to defend my family and birdseed.

The next morning I saw a seagull on our birdfeeder. Was it Jonathon, I wondered? Jonathon was, according to my wife who has a complicated birdseed ownership ethos, eating birdseed that rightfully belonged to yellow finches.

Once again with stealth and practiced calm from being battle-hardened, I fired again. This seagull squawked and was air born. It landed on the roof in front and eyed me maliciously. I crouched, steadied for a long distance shot and fired. The practice paid off. I hit that seagull and he took flight. I still wondered if that was a different seagull or Jonathon.

The next morning, a seagull fed at our bird feeder. I leveled my one good eye with a steely gaze. Eventually, the seagull looked up and our eyes locked.

The seagull squawked loudly, spread his wings and careened into air without me so much as me firing a shot. It indeed had been Jonathon. By protecting my property with Old Blue, I could now vanquish my foe with a glance.

Now I know the true meaning of an eye for an eye.

When I feel agitated or I'm succumbing to the pressures of being retired, I calm my nerves by patrolling our perimeter, and in my hand, faithful Old Blue, my right to do so protected by the United States Constitution's Second Amendment, I'm told.

Another Mancation: In Their Strong Hands

Another mancation, a group of old and young men together for a few days. Late the night we arrive the young men are playing beer pong. Cups of beer sit in the middle of the ping-pong table, one on each side. If the ball hits the cup, the player has to take a drink. If the ball goes in the cup, the player has to drink the entire beer. It's innocent and safe. No one is driving anywhere. Adrenaline and youth keep the young men going. One of the old men has already passed out, and he wasn't even playing.

I'm continually surprised in this youth-centered culture to find the young men return each year. What do these vibrant, thirty-somethings want from us? What could a group of old men have for them? And so I ask.

I like the manly experience, John smiles, then turns serious. I like the outdoors, the high desert country, the camaraderie. You can always learn from someone older. Many shun older people. I don't. Here the heart gets talked about. And the older generation learns from the younger.

Tony is intense. It's worth taking off time from work. Old guys tell good life stories. It's fun. Old guys have a lot of knowledge.

Colby says, I would never fish. I wouldn't know where to go. I don't have the equipment. He rubs his chin philosophically. When my father is with his friends, it's another side of him I would never get to see.

The next day, we're to meet at the river. They're late and full of fire. On the way they've been to a brewery and had an encounter with the police, but everything is all right.

We are showing them how to rig a feathered lure so they might catch a fish from The Crooked River in central Oregon. Someone should have taught them this already.

We hover over them like mothers over daughters off to the prom. I should be able to think of a male analogy but we're old and so behave more like women than men. They make our heart hurt, they are so beautiful. They remind us of what we once were.

The land above us is corrugated cliff upon cliff to three hundred feet, layer on layer of columnar basalt thirty million years old, laid down the way we educate our young, layer over layer of learning over time.

We are bereft of ritual among males in our culture of Kardashians and kickboxing and constant coverage. We used to have ceremonies. We reach into our pouch of magic looking for a charm that will teach them everything we meant to but didn't because we were busy making a living, trying to get more, or whatever we thought was more important at the time. We find nothing but old receipts and ticket stubs.

The rain comes in instantly like tragedy, a quick cold sprinkle with wind that raises chill bumps. The weather change causes fish to rise and suddenly the surface of the river sparkles with fish flash. All the old men bring in trout. Young men nothing. Our stock rises with the fish.

We are far down the path they will walk. We know where the rocks and roots are that can trip them up. We know because we have stumbled over them. We don't want to hand anything over to them, this next generation, like handing off a baton in a relay. We just want to protect them. Besides, they already have taken it from us like each generation takes it. It's all in their strong hands now.

The last day of mancation Colby is watching one of the old ones send an artificial insect across moving water trying to get a trout to rise. I lie back in the grass. The Crooked River whispers its continuous aspirated syllable into my ear. It says, hush.

I can hardly keep my eyes open.

Doesn't Play Well With Others

Unlike Sarah Palin (remember Sarah?) you can't see Alaska from our house, but you can see Cape Kiwanda. Everyone who comes here has an opinion about the Cape. Erosion sure has made it smaller, they inevitably say, hasn't it.

See, it's the *hasn't it* I have a problem with. In the first place when they say *hasn't it,* despite the grammatical construction, it's not a question. *Hasn't it* means if I have any more IQ than an artichoke, I'll agree. They're not asking my opinion.

When was the last time anyone asked your opinion? You have a lot of people, do you, lined up at your front door begging you to tell them if Lady Gaga has gone too far, is the iPhone worth the extra money, who should be allowed to keep singing or dancing, do the Beavers need a new coach, vanilla or chocolate?

I'll bet you have enough opinions, though, don't you? Everyone you meet gives you one, even if you never ask. I had one acquaintance who was always telling me what to think. One day I said, you've got a lot of great opinions. The next time I want one, I'll ask you for it.

I had one exchange - look at that haystack rock. Looks just like King Kong, doesn't it. No, I think it looks more like Gordon Hinckley. Who's Gordon Hinckley? A kid I went to high school with. At this point, I usually get an eye roll.

You never agree with anyone, do you, my wife Joani often observes. No, I reply, I don't, because everyone's usually wrong.

I bought a photo circa 1940 of Cape Kiwanda. I hung it on the wall. If someone had said Cape Kiwanda has changed, I would agree. The distribution of the trees has migrated east.

There are actually more trees than there were. The sand has been covered by vegetation, but it's still there. No, for the most part, Cape Kiwanda is still about the same size. When people declare it's smaller, I grab the photo off the wall, hand it to them and say, prove it.

We should be grateful for contrarians, for people who never agree. We're the ones who nudge us forward, who give the us fresh knowledge, who create and correct our world. Many contrarians end up in politics. Ralph Yarborough, Wayne Morse, Peter de Fazio come to mind. Some write columns. On their report card the plays-well-with-others box was not checked.

When a breakthrough comes, it is attributed to usually one person. The group can't convince the individual. Despite the opposition of the Church and the prevailing theories of the time, Copernicus picked up the Earth from the center of the universe and replaced it with the sun. Einstein took space and time in his hands and bent them into a curve, despite being the only one who thought so. Oregon Senator Wayne Morse disagreeing with virtually the entire Senate said it was a mistake to go to war in Viet Nam. Scott Ritter said there was no evidence of WMD's in Iraq.

Want to be a contrarian? The next time someone asks, don't you think so, pause, think, line up your reasons and state your conclusion.

Say what you think. It's the coin of the realm. It's your worth. Spend it. Of course they'll think you're crazy, and forget getting the plays-well-with-others box checked.

Or perhaps not. They might respect you for standing up for what you believe. They might ask to see a picture of Gordon Hinckley.

Movement is Wealth

I was offered a job recently. Yes, it was a harrowing experience, much like being involved in an automobile accident when everything goes into slow motion, but when I explained I was a writer, I was thrown clear.

The mistake I made was moving around. If I had stayed put like I was supposed to, like most retired people, I would have been safe. When you move around you become susceptible to the laws of nature. It's an unknown fact that one of the laws of nature is, movement creates wealth.

How do you think Marco Polo could afford to travel to China in 1260? Granted, rates were cheaper then, but mainly it was his father, who paid for everything, which is another law of nature. A young man probably pops into your cerebral cortex right now who would surely die of lack of Doritos and video games if left to his own resources. Have you considered sending him to China? Like Marco Polo he could go into the pasta business and return as a representative of the Top Ramen Corporation.

Anyway, Marco Polo's father didn't pay for everything all the time. Marco met Kublai Khan who paid for everything. Unfortunately that's like having the Mafia pay for everything. They're going to want something in return. As it turned out, Emperor Khan wanted holy oil from the Vatican. See? One day you're sitting at home wishing pasta had been invented and the next day your life is a Dan Brown novel.

My point is, if you're bored and a little short of wealth, there is an easy answer – road trip!

Why are Muleshoe, Texas and Bullshirt Springs, Oregon (recently renamed), not worldwide commercial centers and New York, Singapore, and Cloverdale (I saw it on a tee shirt) are? Simple. They can afford to hire Weiden and Kennedy, the famous Portland PR firm, plus they're located at the intersection of well-established trade routes created by the Kardashians, an ancient shopping family.

People who are older than you want to give you advice. Listen to us. If Ben in that movie The Graduate had listened when that friend of his father tried to give him career advice in one word, plastics, he would have gone to work the next day and avoided sitting on the bottom of his swimming pool in scuba gear showing how symbolically superior he was to everyone over thirty and a complicated plot that so confused him he didn't know whether to have an affair with Mrs. Robinson or her daughter so he did both. He also would have been able to grow into middle age drinking expensive scotch and have nothing to say to his kids except single words of advice like internet.

If you remember the last job you had, most likely you got it because you were out moving about. I know, I know, the way people really get jobs today is monster.com. You go on line to submit a resume while your avatar is being attacked by dragons, a sort of video game for the unemployed.

Okay, so you weren't actually moving yourself about but moving your avatar about. Since job hunting today doesn't involve showing up in a real office with plants where they can smell how many times you've worn that shirt, and since they meet your avatar instead, it's important to have an impressive avatar, somewhere between Beyonce and Brad Pitt. Your problem is your avatar is more like Charlie Brown.

So work on your avatar, network with friends and listen to the older generation. We know a lot. Besides, with the bang up job we've done for the past couple decades, I'm sure you'll want to be just like us.

The Eyes Have It

So, what do you think, my new headshot, at the top of the page? Pretty cool, eh? Two eyes. One's fake. This column is about eyes.

My friend Ielean has great vision. She can spot a Japanese glass fishing float embedded in a pile of kelp a hundred beachcombers missed on a busy weekend. She infers I don't have the best vision only because I use the Braille driving method.

No part of the human body generates so much emotion as the eyes. It's visceral, meaning you can feel it in your gut. Want an example? Sometimes an eye doctor, an ophthalmologist, has to give a patient a shot in the side of the eyeball. One is not permitted to use hypodermic needle and eye in the same sentence. I can feel your shoulders shiver from here.

If you have 20/20 vision, it doesn't mean it's perfect. It means you have average vision. You can see at twenty feet what the average person can see at twenty feet. An optometrist told my sister at a vision check to read the bottom line on the eye chart. She has 20/10 vision. She read, Product of the American Optometrist Society.

What's this obsession we have with eyes? The eyes are the windows to the soul, poets insist. Pres. Bush looked into Vladimir Putin's eyes and said he saw his soul. It must have been a very big soul to block the view of a dozen political opponents and journalists he's had assassinated. If you think you can look into someone's eyes and tell if they're lying, I have an investment opportunity for you. Any sociopath or lawyer can lie convincingly while holding eye contact. It's required in sales. Have I offended everyone yet?

There are more sayings about the eyes than any other part of the body. Clear-eyed. Evil eye. Roving eye. All eyes. Bedroom eyes. Gandhi said an eye for an eye leaves the whole world blind.

Remember the first time you fell in love? It took somewhere between two to three seconds, and it was all done with your eyes. Try it, sustained eye contact with a stranger, best not with your spouse around or with a Hells Angel.

So what's happening in those three seconds when we fall in love? Forget the romantic schema dreamed up by that big fat wrinkly forebrain we're so proud of, the cerebral cortex, which comes up with a brilliant idea that involves a heart-shaped box of candy or a Leatherman. This is a much more primitive part of the gray matter at work, the hypothalamus, the part of your brain that grunts, interested in eating and sex. In those three seconds when your eyes are locked, it's assessing health, body parts, hips, chest, the gloss of the hair, and the eyes. If the eyes are clear and aligned, it's an indicator of overall good health, meaning if you make babies, they won't be deformed.

Male or female, this is not a pickup line that will work in a bar. But in essence it's the same process a dairy would use to select breeding stock. A dairy person of the female persuasion told me recently, when she checks a milk cow, for an adult, she looks for high, perky teats. For a younger one, she examines the butt for diarrhea.

I am in no way inferring you should use this method to pick a potential mate, but it's an unknown fact when you make eyes at someone, this is what your primitive brain is doing.

Besides, I don't think Hallmark makes a card for it.

Zombies Have Shut Down the Government

At least when I wrote this. What is it with the zombies? It's like all zombies all the time now. What is a zombie, anyway? There are all sorts of zombie lore. It is said in voodoo legend that feeding a zombie salt will make it return to the grave. In some communities it is believed that a dead person can be turned into a zombie by a small child. I've had a small child and I can tell you after three days without sleep I was a zombie.

Zombie fiction is now a sizeable sub-genre of horror fiction, occurring when most of the population becomes flesh-eating zombies, a zombie apocalypse. Zombies have appeared as plot devices in various books, films, television shows, video games and comics and seems to show up as an objective correlative symbolizing a breakdown of civilization.

We found out recently that if you try to leave a little kid in a graveyard late at night, he'll freak out, even if you offer to leave him a gun to protect himself. Why? It's because on some instinctual level, all humans know it's just a matter of time until the zombies show up. Turns out there is a very good reason this is happening.

Parasites that turn victims into mindless, zombie-like slaves are fairly common in nature. There's one called toxoplasmosa gondii that seems to devote its entire existence to infecting rats, but can only breed inside the intestines of a cat. The parasite knows it needs to get the rat inside the cat so the parasite takes over the rat's brain, and intentionally makes it scurry toward where the cats hang out. The rat is being programmed to get itself eaten, and it doesn't even know.

If you're comforting yourself with the thought that it may take forever for such a parasite to evolve, you're forgetting about all the biological weapons programs around the world, intentionally weaponizing such bugs. You've got to wonder if the lab workers don't carry out their work under the unwitting command of the toxoplasmosa gondii already in their brains.

Of course, those are just rats, right? How it can result in zombies? Did I mention it's an unknown fact half the human population on Earth is infected with toxoplasmosis? Maybe you're one of them. Flip a coin.

Scientific studies have shown that the infected see a change in their personality and have a higher chance of exhibiting signs of mental illness like running for public office.

So what are the chances this could cause a zombie apocalypse? Humans and rats share many similarities. That's why rats are used to test our drugs. All it takes is a more evolved version of toxoplasmosa gondii, one that could do to us what it does to the rats. So, imagine if half the world suddenly had no instinct for self-preservation or rational thought, even less than they do now. Let's assume half of those in Congress were infected.

You may be protesting that technically these people have never been dead and thus don't fit the dictionary definition of "zombies." We can assure you that the distinction doesn't matter a whole lot since these groaning hordes may not yet be clawing their way through your windows, but they're already being interviewed on TV political news shows. Besides, this obsession over details is a symptom you might be infected.

That's exactly the behavior politicians are exhibiting. Everyone is worried about their own details while the government is burning. We notice zombies even now are exhaling their way into the regular news, whatever that is, stories devoid of Miley Cyrus or Rhianna, I suppose.

A zombie is a term used to describe a hypnotized person bereft of consciousness and self-awareness. Sound like anyone you voted for?

Don't bother waiting for the zombie apocalypse. It's here.

What's Your Mission?

What does your mission statement say? What do you mean you don't have a mission statement? How do you know what you're supposed to do if you don't have a mission statement?

I have a mission statement for everything, even marriage. Come to think of it, especially marriage. My mission statement for marriage is, stay married. You'd be amazed at the lack of thinking required to stay married if you follow your mission statement. For instance, when that attractive young woman at the bar asks what that cologne is I'm wearing, and come to think of it that hasn't happened for some time because young people nowadays are so into themselves, I remember my mission statement and respond, Old Spice for The Aged. Actually, I don't think she said what's that cologne. It might have been, what's that smell.

Rosanne Barr, the comedian, had a mission statement for raising kids. She said, if the children are still alive when my husband comes home, I've done my job.

Rosanne was right, according to sociobiologists Dawkins, Pinker and Wilson who said research shows that heredity, DNA, over which you have no control is ninety-eight percent responsible for your son singing like Brad Pitt and looking like Willie Nelson. The two percent your affect has on your offspring in the nature vs. nurture debate is the ability to achieve a high kill rate in Mortal Kombat and the tendency to set fire to schools.

Most of you don't realize you have a shopping mission statement. You foolishly think it's something like, through the hawk-eyed technique of applying every coupon ever printed in newspapers to stretch your shopping dollars, you'll have money left for essentials like medical care and cable.

Wrong.

If you delve deeply into your unconscious you'll find your actual shopping mission statement is to endure rice casseroles until your bimonthly trip to Costco where, in a state of giddiness, your lunch for the day consists of three dozen small paper cups of food substitutes whose chemicals distort your thought processes to the point it seems reasonable to trade in the vehicle you're driving on a truck big enough to haul the bales of paper products and the dryer that was on sale.

At the risk of being perceived as sexist, men have a shelter mission statement. It goes something like this – through the use of my labor, to improve the domicile for my family to better ensure their comfort and safety.

Your unconscious mission statement goes more like this – to purchase enough power tools to equal the cost of the project so you can do it yourself, saving enough to have it ripped out and done right by a professional.

Be grateful the newspaper you're reading this very instant doesn't have the usual journalistic mission statement, if it bleeds, it leads, but the mission statement we've all come to know and love, all kids and cows all the time.

Of course we've got one mission statement left to consider. It's the big one. Philosophy and religion, it's all they talk about. Why are we here? What's the purpose of my life? What's the meaning of it all? How does Groupon work?

You're on your own on this one, Sparky. You could read the great thinkers. You could go to church.

A few words of observation. You can delegate strategies. You can delegate actions. You can't delegate responsibility. If someone tells you to treat others badly, it's a dead giveaway. Bad mission statement. Treating all races, religions, genders and their preference, conducting your private life the way you want to as long as you're not violating the Big Mission Statement, it's a good start.

The Big Mission Statement? Oh, come on. You know it. It's the basis for all the others.

Do unto others.

The Scariest Beast

Happy Halloween! When I was a child I dressed like Richard Nixon to scare the Democrats and went through the neighborhood, gathering enough high-fructose corn syrup for MacDonald's to construct 365 Happy Meals.

Although most Christians claim Halloween, the holiday is commonly thought to have pagan roots, originally called Samhain from the Celtic, meaning Summer's End. Prior to that, it was the Roman festival of the dead called Parentalia, generating the phrase, careful, your parentalia are showing.

Halloween is a financially important holiday second only to Santa Day. You can tell Halloween is coming, if not from the commercials in May, then in September by the number of salmon fishers at the boat ramp.

Halloween imagery includes themes of death, evil the occult, and mythical creatures like liberal Republicans. The modern imagery of Halloween are pumpkins, corn husks, and scarecrows. New scary visages have worked their way into national consciousness and are used to frighten conservatives, liberals, and children like Obama, Palin and Trump.

Also, this was a time for taking stock and preparing for the cold winter ahead. Halloween was seen as a time when the door to the otherworld opened. Souls of the dead and Tinkerbell could come into our world which is thought to have influenced today's Halloween customs, like wearing costumes as a means of hiding from these harmful spirits, and us from our neighbors, an unknown fact, the origin of the KKK.

It marked the beginning of winter or the darker half of the year. We humans have a darker half, marked by bonfires and human sacrifice, like Hitler did with the Jews, Hutu/Tutsi did with each other, and our Pilgrims, Davy Crockett and a dozen or more U. S. Presidents did with the American aborigines, already here when we showed up.

I know what you're thinking. It's hard to build a bonfire on a subway staging area, but it is apparently easy to, as a woman did a short time ago, push a man to his death in front of a subway train because he was "Muslim or Hindu and 911." It was the second such incident in a month. The man was neither, but you're missing the point. She was just practicing our heritage. Maybe you could celebrate Halloween and your heritage this year by pushing your boss in front of a train.

We've always had ghoulish practices. The Chinese broke the feet of their six-year-old girls so they could bind them and force four of their toes to touch their heels, leaving only the great toe on which to walk, causing the death of one in ten of them due to infections. If you'd like an example a little closer to home, our very own Tillamook Indians, think Flatheads, thought they could make babies more beautiful than when they were born by strapping them to boards to flatten their heads, causing a large number to go blind.

Lest you shake your head in smugness at these barbaric practices, we have our own we still practice today.. We tell women they're most beautiful when they cram their toes into pointed shoes, forcing their heels high in the air, their breasts forward, their buttocks back and foot, leg and back injury to the six out of ten women who wear high heels.

If we really want to sacrifice a group, have we considered Congress? No one I know would object.

If the human species wants to see the scariest beast of all, more frightening than anything Hollywood could come up with, worse than Freddy, worse than Chucky, worse than

Hannibal Lector, Norman Bates or Bashir Assad, it just has to take off its Halloween mask and look in the mirror.

I'll see you at the plaza. Don't forget your pitchfork and torch.

Boo.

The Art of Short Relationships

I would be a standup comedian except that I'm slow-witted. If I were heckled on stage my idea of a retort would be, oh yeah?

If there are any wannabe stand-ups in my reading audience, I've got a great idea for a bit for you. Short relationships. I don't mean the kind of short relationships I had when I was dating in first grade. My new friend Bill Brown, in the first grade everything was new since preschool hadn't been invented yet, came up to me and said, I've got a girlfriend. You do? How did you get a girl friend? Bill explained, I just asked.

I turned away from Bill Brown in the lunch line and there she was, Linda Clark, beautiful and convenient. Will you be my girlfriend, I asked. Linda Clark took a step back, looked me up and down and said, okay. I turned to Bill Brown. I've got a girlfriend, too.

Over my shoulder I heard my new girlfriend say to the girl next to her, I have a boyfriend, looks like a monkey.

That's not the kind of short relationship I'm talking about. I'm talking about the kind you have in the checkout line or in an elevator, keeping in mind in order to have a short relationship in an elevator you'd have to leave Tillamook County.

You have short relationships all the time, the tow truck driver who rescues you, the nurse who stabs you with a needle, the attendant at the gas station. I try to keep in mind I'm being served by another human being.

One doesn't have a lot of latitude of action to have a short relationship in an elevator. The relationship consists mainly of facing the same direction, keeping your mouth shut, and trying not to share your methane.

It's much easier to have a short relationship in a checkout line. To that end I'd just like to warn you, no matter how virtuous you might feel because you have brought a dozen recyclable grocery bags to the register, no matter how much you feel our earth's very survival as a planet depends on just you, checkers don't like them. In fact, they hate them and they hate you and your children because you use them. They have to examine each one to use it. They especially don't appreciate you trying to salvage one with a broken handle by tying one of the pieces to the other handle, rendering the opening so small it's impossible to put anything inside larger than a lemon.

More advice. You can't joke about someone's job. They won't get it. If in response to the checker's question, did you find everything, I say, I couldn't find the dinosaur eggs, she will send a clerk to get me a dozen dinosaur eggs and when she finds out I was joking, she won't give me the sale price on anything.

I was checking out and my checker repeated her line mechanically, find everything, a computerized voice. I started to say something to lighten the mood, and then I noticed her mouth was clamped and I could see the muscles in her temple.

Hard day? I asked. What? she asked, startled. Has it been a hard day? Our eyes locked. She paused checking. Her eyes went red and brimmed. She resumed checking, nodded and said, a very hard day.

She folded the slip, handed me my change, and without looking said, thanks for shopping with us today, Mr. Moore. I leaned in and said, tomorrow will be better. She looked up, her face blank.

I started the car, looked out my left window for the mirror to back out, and there she was. I rolled down the window.

You dropped this, she said and handed me a twenty. Before I could respond, she said, thanks.

Dogs and Husbands – The Training Challenge

Someone asked me recently, you don't like pets, do you, Schubert? Of course I like pets. It's pet owners I don't like.

More accurately, I don't like what happens to my friends when they get a pet. They lose IQ. Case in point, Poopsie-woopsie, ask Schubie-woobie if he wants some coffee. Another case in point, Americans spent $350M on Halloween costumes for their pets this year.

Bringing reality into a conversation about pets is like commenting on a woman's weight. It's a bad idea. If you're a man and you have a fraction of the sense God gave a worm, you will never say anything about a woman's weight. Same with pets, not that I'm inferring anything by mentioning women and pets in the same column. How do I get out of this? See what I'm talking about? Bad idea.

According to John Bradshaw, director of the Anthrozoology Institute at the University of Bristol in the U.K., who has spent much of his career debunking bad advice given to dog owners in his book Dog Sense, your dog is not a wolf nor a furry human who likes to walk on four legs, nor is it vying for dominance

Bradshaw said your dog's job is to be more self-reliant than an adult and better behaved than a child, meaning more mature than a husband. Since we frequently leave dogs alone, your job is to teach your dog how to be alone. You do that by having the same routine, getting your keys from the same place, going out, staying for ten seconds, and coming in. Repeat by staying longer each time. Soon your dog will ignore you just like a husband. When you come back, make a fuss over your dog so it associates you leaving with pleasure like a husband does.

I tried this technique with my son. I sent him outside to play, each time longer than the last to get him used to being away from us, ignoring his comments that no one ever came to look for him, or that it was raining.

Even though dogs are colorblind and have a small advantage hearing in the upper tones it is their nose that is amazing. Between two identical swimming pools, a dog can tell which one has had added a teaspoon of sugar, but it can't tell you why someone would add sugar to a swimming pool.

I think dogs have a right to sniff things, Bradshaw asserts. When I meet a dog I hold my hand out. Not doing so, he says, is like meeting someone while covering your face.

I agree with Bradshaw in principle, but I didn't hold out my nether region to be sniffed at a recent dinner party and if their German shepherd can smell a teaspoon of sugar in a swimming pool, why did it need to contact my crotch intimately with it's nose under the dining room table at a friend's house during the salad course so that I mistook it for the redhead across the table playing footsie. Good thing I didn't return the favor. I would have had to cover my face.

One of the most common problems owners face, says Bradshaw, is knowing what to do when a dog misbehaves. For example, many owners might be inclined to immediately and physically reprimand a dog for that classic embarrassing moment, humping a visitor's leg, but, Bradshaw says, that's the wrong way. They see any form of attention, even negative attention, as a reward. Instead, he says, owners should look away immediately and pretend the dog isn't in the same room, ignoring them, arms crossed. The same should work with a husband.

You'll find that quite quickly the dog or husband will get the idea what it's not supposed to do when friends come to visit.

The Art of Doing Nothing

My long scythe whispered and left the hay to make – Robert Frost.

Know when to stop – Lao Tse.

When our son Josh was just crawling, he pushed open the screen door, crawled half way through, changed his mind and tried to back up. Stuck. He growled, he yelled, he screamed. I watched. He stopped, thought, and pushed through, crawling to me, grinning.

Scientists tried to control coyotes in Eastern Oregon by poisoning them. With fewer coyotes, their food source, rabbits, exploded, exploding the population of coyotes.

We planted European beach grass to stabilize the sand that used to obscure the roads at Kiwanda. It stabilized the sand into a 150-ft. high ridge that blocked views, built a twenty-foot sand cliff on the spit three miles long that harbored predators which ran off snowy plovers, and occasionally collapses, killing teenagers, and so on.

The State of Oregon wanted to make a safe entry port out of Tillamook Bay. It did. It also changed the ocean currents, which destroyed the town of Bay Ocean.

We've tried to protect the salmon by killing and harassing sea lions and birds that have been feeding on salmon smolts since God was a kid. We've spent millions raising hatchery salmon with no proof they help the native species they're designed to strengthen.

We've acted to protect the spotted owl, which increased the population of barred owls, which eat spotted owls. We brought the eagle, the symbol of our country's strength, back from DDT-caused near extinction, a bird, I've seen bullied and the fish it was eating stolen by two seagulls.

We've brought water to the cities by creating deserts.

Our attempts to feed our nation has resulted in a kind of starvation on empty calories, creating an epidemic of obesity. We filled the supermarkets with pool ball tomatoes and destroyed the family garden. In our search for health we've declared cream, eggs, and bread the enemy. We've so distorted beef it has to be fed antibiotics to live which create germs that kill us.

We fought World War I we named the war to end all wars. It led to World War II. We created the United Nations to resolve conflicts and told it to sit down and shut up when it tells us we're a bully.

It's difficult to count the number of American soldiers killed by weapons we've given to rebel groups we're trying to help.

We, the richest country in the world, are joined at the computer to the rest of the world and our economic welfare threatened by, why not, Greece and Iceland.

We supply the money both to fight the war on drugs and the market to keep it in business. There are young men serving long sentences related to marijuana who, when they are released, will be able to go to a State operated store to buy some.

We created Earth Day in 1970, and since, evicted the polar bears with no forwarding address by melting the arctic ice cap of the only planet we've got.

Fathers love their sons so much they use strict discipline on them so they'll turn into fine men who avoid their fathers.

It's easy to connect the dots from Lao Tse to Frost. They said the same things. Know when to act. Know when to stop.

Or, think more, do less.

A Thanksgiving Reminder

Thanksgiving is here and you might remind yourself it takes your village to tell you what time it is.

One time in my life I did research for a project by volunteering in what was at the time called a nursing home by spending a couple of hours a day talking with Helen.

She had advanced arthritis. She couldn't move her arms or legs without help, which meant she couldn't scratch her nose if it itched. Helen had relatives nearby. They never visited. In essence, Helen had been abandoned.

Before I started, I told the person in charge why I was there and I wouldn't be there long. She said, I don't care why you're here. You're here. Most have no one. A little is better than nothing.

Helen was lost in time. She didn't know when this was. When I look at a calendar, she said, it's like it's written in a code I can't break.

I know what you're thinking, Alzheimer, dementia. You're wrong. Helen was as lucid as anyone. She could discuss any subject, politics, music, as long as her place in time was not a factor. She had been a concert pianist of some note. Particularly cruel, you might think, considering her situation.

Helen gave me a gift. She helped me see into a dual mystery, that meaning and time are functions of each other, the same way altitude and barometric pressure are co-functions, and neither exist outside the village.

I can see your eyes glaze over. Stay with me.

Helen was eighty-three. I was forty. Once she asked, did you know my father? Using brute logic she realized she had asked a silly question. Forgive me, she said, closing her eyes. You couldn't have known my father.

Time and meaning are human constructs. Outside of the human brain, they don't exist. Even God would agree with that. No one except those on industrial medication would suggest the planet Jupiter spends a lot of time thinking about what things mean. As far as we know, only we do that.

Let's say you're at the movies. Choose your gender role for this example. A woman sits next to a man. The comic on the screen points at his sidekick's unzipped pants and laughs. On impulse the man sitting in the dark glances down and in the reflected light from the screen, sees his pants zipper is open. Keeping his eyes on the screen, he zips up.

When the house lights come up he stands to realize the woman's full skirt next to him is caught in his zipper.

A month later, the man backs into a car. It's the same woman. He finds she's his boss' wife.

This makes for a great story you can tell and retell at gatherings.

Unless you go to no gathering. Unless you're totally alone. Then the story begins to lose its meaning. It doesn't mean anything because you can't use it to entertain because there is no one to entertain.

No one really cares whether you were embarrassed, lost your job, or had an affair because no one will ever know about it.

As the events themselves begin to lose their importance, so do their order. If the events become meaningless, does it really matter which one comes first?

Time then hisses out like an ember dropped into a lagoon.

Helen told me of the events of her life, not as a connected web, but as discreet particles, like grains of salt on a tabletop.

After three months, I left Helen. I would like to say the demands my circle of friends, my work, raising my family didn't leave me any time, but that wouldn't be the truth. I simply couldn't do it any more. I couldn't make myself go into that place again.

This Thanksgiving, maintain your friendships. Reach out to others. Keep your village in good repair. You don't want to find yourself out of time.

Mr. News Guy Explains Cats and Dogs

It's time once again for Mr. News Guy to explain trends in the news. What are they, Mr. News Guy?

Cats. Cats dominate YouTube and run several large corporations.

Mr. News Guy, cats have come a long way from the job of catching mice to the job of making us feel inferior. This presents some problems since cats haven't had the time to evolve to their new role. Instead of helping us establish an inferiority complex by ignoring us, they present us with a bloody mouse and then ignore us.

You're upstaging me.

Mr. News Guy. Do cats love us?

That's not the question you want to ask. A decent interviewer would ask do you want your cat to love you like a dog. How would you like it if when you came home in the evening, your cat Pywacket wagged its tail back and forth while grinning stupidly, leapt repeatedly into the air like a maniac while slobbering over a tennis ball it wanted you to throw, and unable to maintain attention span, attacked and swallowed your slipper?

You didn't answer the question, Mr. News Guy.

You can be replaced. It would be hard to tell if a cat loved you. Cats evolved as a solitary hunter while dogs evolved from a pack. Getting dogs to party would be like taking a keg to a frat house. Partying with a cat would be like trying to get a ninja drunk.

No point in being derogatory, Mr. News Guy. What does a cat's purr mean?

Amazing, You used a five-syllable word. You're probably trying to ask what a cat's purr means. Some experts say it's an expression of affection while others claim it's just seeking your warmth and wants you to feed it while imagining what it would do if the situation were reversed and it were fifteen times larger than you.

Mr. News Guy, there is an issue making the news right now. The number of songbirds is falling due to cats.

You seem to have an anti-cat bias. Mr. and Mrs. or Mr. and Mr. or Mrs. and Mrs. or whatever, are out for an evening walk with Billy or Susie and a cat leaps on a yellow goldfinch and looks up proudly with a couple of yellow feathers sticking to its mouth expecting you to compliment it on doing what a cat is supposed to do, a perfectly executed decapitation. Instead, the parents express horror and cover their kid's eyes.

Guh-ross, Mr. News Guy, and I don't think it's necessary to insult the LGBT community.

Obviously you're a dog person. The next thing that happens involves teaching their kid what happened was bad, forcing them to write letters to their senators and marching on the street corner with homemade signs.

That's, what should happen, you haughty cat person.

Have the courtesy to address me as Mr. News Guy. What should happen is they should get a life. What should happen is they should try to explain the difference in a cat killing a bird and the baby cows used to make veal Parmesan or where it is exactly we get lamb or bacon or McDonalds get Happy Meals. Good luck with that.

You've heard of the term herding cats? You can't train a cat to do anything, whereas a dog can be trained to save lives and...

Of course cats can be trained, you imbecile. Mother cats train their kittens when not to use their claws by making a sound of extreme disapproval, a type of fake-spitting, like this, ACK! ACK!

That cat should have been declawed.

What?! Declawed?! Declawing is mutilation! It's like cutting your fingers off! It's illegal in Europe!

This isn't Europe. All cats should be declawed. It would be rough, but for the best. Yes, rough, rough.

ACK! ACK!

One Hunter's Ethic

The first time I ever killed a living thing I was ten years old and shot a rabbit with a .410 shotgun. My father made me skin and gut the furry creature. Ew, I said. My father was a man of few words. He said, hunters aren't allowed to say, ew.

My father never told me it's all right to kill game if you eat it. I came to that belief through the act of pulling the fir off the purple body of that rabbit, of emptying its organs on the earth. I became connected to that rabbit, felt emotions new to me for it, and wasn't aware that my emotions constructed an ethic on the spot.

I washed the body of the rabbit after gutting and laid it on clean paper. My new ethic whispered in my ear, this, sir, is the way you should treat the game you kill. And above all, do not waste it.

My mother fried the rabbit and we ate it for dinner. It was a visceral belief in my budding hunting ethic that if I had not eaten that rabbit it would have been a sin.

It didn't make any logical sense, but it made perfect emotional sense that it was the same way I would want to have been treated, if it were I who was hunted, shot and gutted, similar to the way we treat in death members of our own species, except, of course, the frying and eating part.

In my ethic, fishing is hunting, and I'm not so much a fisher as a cook who fishes. I've launched my dory through the surf at Pacific City/Cape Kiwanda to go out in the Pacific to catch the freshest fish for dinner. I thought of it as free food until my wife did a disservice to my fun by dividing how much I'd spent on boat, motor, gear and repairs by the number of fish I'd caught. You don't know pressure until your spouse tells you, no, I don't mind you going fishing at all. Just don't come home empty handed.

I built a metal-weighted club that ends life instantly, or perhaps consciousness, and I do so as a direct result of that first rabbit I shot. With that club I have rendered still, thirty-pound tuna with one blow preventing their death throes and spraying blood in a wide arc. Chefs would chuckle and point out that's not why fish are clubbed. They would say you club a fish to prevent stress enzymes from adversely affecting the quality of the meat. You do it for your reasons. I'll do it for mine.

Once fishing for halibut and skunked, I caught a hundred-and-fifty-pound skate. It took three of us to bring it into my dory. Skate was the main entrée at Paley's Place, the winner of best restaurant in Portland that year.

It filled the deck. It was so large my club was useless against its great, hard body. Finally, we cut off the wings, which I was told were the only edible parts and let the rest of it, still alive, slip away back into the sea.

I vowed I would never do that again. Although I'm not a vegetarian, I say to those of you who are, you don't have to make your case to me. I understand.

I violated my ethic with that skate. I couldn't render it unconscious. There was so little of it I used, so much wasted. I'm a skilled cook. I prepared and served it with a cucumber remoulade. Everyone raved. I took one bite and could eat no more.

I imagine some great fisher pulling me up from the depths. He has an ethic much like mine, which would compel him to render me unconscious and would not look me eye-to-eye, say ew, and let me slip away.

Fame – A Cruel Mistress

Even though we're tucked away in the upper left-hand corner of the map and have gone as far west as we can without getting our feet wet, we're still connected to the rest of the world through the screens we stare at, and I'll tell you I'm worried about the poor people in the news.

Being a local celebrity, I understand the pressure for the requests to make an appearance, for my autograph, the paparazzi, who, after seeing my photo in the HH every week, figure that's enough.

I'm worried that Miley Cyrus' family gatherings might get a little tense when she starts giving her father Billy Ray career advice after he makes too many trips to the punchbowl and breaks into another rendition of Achy Breaky Heart when she points out one hit isn't enough to sustain a career and he needs to twerk.

I'm worried the relationship between Mrs. Gaga and Lady will be strained because Mrs. Gaga will act like any mom and keep reminding Lady who she is which she needs to do because I have no idea who her daughter is from one performance to the next unless I see the credits on the screen.

I'm worried about the motivation of the lower level Al Qaeda members. I mean, what with drones taking out the leaders, who wants to get promoted? Their spelling, too. Who uses a Q without a U?

I'm afraid Gov. Chris Christie is using Rush Limbaugh as a weight loss consultant. I'm afraid we underestimate the effectiveness of Vice President Joe Biden who was sent to calm things down with China who will agree to practically anything if Joe will just quit talking and go home.

I'm concerned about The Rolling Stones and The Pope. Even though the Pope has six years on Mick and he doesn't play guitar like Mick doesn't and he doesn't have any recordings in the top 100, I'm told he's a rock star and Mick doesn't need the competition and I don't want the Pope to forget what his real job is.

I'm worried about Toronto Mayor Ron Ford. Crack is a gateway drug to what, Drano?

I'm worried what with a third of young people saying they get their news from Jon Stewart's The Daily Show, Jon will get confused trying to tell the difference between his show and the real news.

I'm apprehensive that despite being one of the most effective Secretaries of State, able to put up with Bill for all these years, and being convinced to run for President of the United States, Hillary will overlook the fact that women just don't like her.

I'm worried that Bruce Jenner, father of two or more interchangeable daughters, Kardashians, famous for large body parts, won't be able to tell his daughters apart and will never figure out what it is they do.

I'm afraid Justin Bieber will lose his fans when his voice changes, George Clooney will end a perfect life by getting married, Mike Tyson will try to act, sing, or do anything, Robert De Niro will make another comedy, Barbra Streisand will direct another movie, Kevin Costner or Sandra Bullock will act in another movie and Charlize Theron won't. I'm afraid Oprah will lose the love of her fans by running for office.

I'm afraid with the example of Nelson Mandela to inspire him, President Obama will have his heart broken by attempting a greater feat than ending apartheid in South Africa, working with the United States Congress.

And locally, I'm worried incisive political analyst and respected journalist for the Headlight Herald, Joe Wrabek, will give in to a groundswell of support demanding he run for something. He will then find out, like I did, what a cruel mistress fame can be.

Time to Set Fire to the Christmas Tree

Everyone knows the origin of Christmas, the mass celebrating the birthday of baby Jesus. How, you might be wondering, did all this other stuff get added to Bethlehem, a date-eating desert town, like peppermint sticks and spray-on snow? Unlike my usual practice, I'm making none of this up. We either invented it over a long period of time like Santa Claus which started out as the pagan god Odin and then was added to and modified by songs, poems, and the Coco Cola Company, but is still a pretty weird figure for a religious day.

Or if we're tired we just grab something cool from any handy culture, like the origin of the Christmas tree which we think is pretty naked without a maddening string of electric lights and glass balls which symbolize burning candles which symbolized the stars Martin Luther saw shining through the branches of a fir tree, a nice story that never happened but the truth is even cooler, which is the Druids wrapped a fir tree with the festive intestines of their enemies and set fire to the whole thing.

The story of Santa makes me happy. It's what we do best, basic storytelling, adding and changing, the way we tell our personal stories, where the goal is not so much accuracy as a good time. A reindeer whose nose glows in the dark and saves the day invented by a country western singer? Why not?

Take the traditional Christmas dinner. What about a turkey says Christmas? If you have a teenage daughter she's probably asking, aren't we still eating turkey leftovers from Thanksgiving?

She would have prepared herself by googling and would say something like, Mom, as a cook, doesn't this show a lack of imagination on your part? Shouldn't turkey be the traditional

Christmas dinner of, well, Turkey, which was mistakenly named Turkey because the guinea fowl was mistaken for the turkey so the guinea fowl traders were mistakenly called turkey traders like America was mistakenly called India because the GPS hadn't been invented yet?

It's at his point Mom opens the traditional Christmas wine a little early.

Maybe you're a little tired of turkey. Maybe you'd like to have what some of the rest of the world is having.

In France the Christmas dinner is snails or bloated liver of goose, take your pick. In Nigeria you're going to need your live goat. In Austria, fried carp. Iceland, roast reindeer (You can have the punchline. If you're too tired, how about, I'm sorry, Blitzen. We had a lottery. You lost.).

In Sweden, gelatinous, strong-smelling lye fish. In Portugal, salted cod, Romania, pork organs, Slovakia, garlic waffles, Mexico, pig intestine soup. In China the traditional Christmas dinner will be served at Kentucky Fried Chicken. Maybe roast turkey is not sounding so bad.

I remember one Christmas in particular I cooked a Christmas goose. I should have suspected something when I found it at the bottom of the store's freezer and identified it by knocking the frost off so I could read the label. I was wrongly warned to prick the skin a thousand times or it would be so greasy we'd gag. I now know the meaning of when my goose is cooked.

An ice storm had rendered everyone I knew immobile. Sunlight shining through glazed branches spread ten thousand tiny rainbows on the ice crust. We had a fire in the fireplace. Our ten-year-old had toys. I had been given three thousand pages of the Dune anthology. If you put enough gravy on, even dry goose is good.

This was before social media. My wife and I were at peace. We found we didn't speak much that day. We didn't need to. All the traditions we needed were in our house.

We hope yours is, too.

Shame, Embarrassment & Guilt – Counselors

A New Year's resolution is a promise you make to yourself in late December you won't keep so you can hate yourself during the coming year.

Like everything else, resolutions have a religious origin. The ancient Babylonians made promises to their gods at the start of each year that they would return borrowed objects and pay their debts, a practice, by the way I would like to recommend to some people I know.

In the Medieval era, the knights took the "peacock vow" at the end of the Christmas season each year to re-affirm their commitment to chivalry and plumage. Knights have always been vain, which explains the love of big hats by their descendants, cowboys.

Resolutions are kept with the aid of your village, your support group, and shame, embarrassment and guilt, which is not a group of dour counselors. Even though Christians are pretty good in the guilt department and have Lent to take all the fun out of life, the Jews got there first with a double whammy of Rosh Hashanah and Yom Kippur to reflect upon one's wrongdoings over the year and both seek and offer enough forgiveness to make Catholics green with envy.

At the end of the Great Depression, about 25% of Americans adults made New Year's resolutions. At the start of the 21st century, about 40% made them, which might be a big improvement except the 8% that actually keep them has stayed the same.

One example of a resolution is to donate to the poor more often, but after the last five years, uh, that would be you. I'm supposed to become more environmentally responsible, but I have no clue how separating green wine bottles from brown is going to save the planet.

I looked at a list of resolutions my wife recommended. They are eat healthy, lose weight, exercise more, drink less, quit smoking, get out of debt, be less grumpy, get organized, learn a foreign language, make new friends and laugh more. I told her if I did all those I would laugh less. She told me I wasn't supposed to do them all.

New Year's resolutions have changed. At the end of the 19th century, a typical teenage girl focused on good works. Today she wants better hair.

When you think about it, when you make a resolution you are attempting no less than to change who you are. That's a pretty big order. You got to be the way you are because you like it. A cold beer, lasagna, and pecan pie taste better than rice cakes or styrofoam.

You need to enlist your village and shame, embarrassment and guilt. It's the most effective motivation for personal change ever discovered. You need your village, which are your relatives, friends, enemies (enemies are particularly effective), coworkers, church, AA, and any other support group you can think of. Tell them what you want to accomplish, weight loss, stop drinking, stop biting your nails, whatever, and get a partner who wants the same goal. Weight Watchers has built a huge moneymaking business out of shame, embarrassment and guilt. If you doubt this, attend a weigh-in. Tell everyone you know what your goal is. Take out an ad in the paper.

Talk to your partner daily. Call and say, I'm thinking about biting my nails. Have a piece of pie instead, your partner will tell you. Better yet, come over and we'll both have a piece of pie together because I was thinking of biting my nails, too.

Later when you've stopped biting your nails, you can join Weight Watchers.

Gullible, my wife said, add that to your list of suggestions for your resolutions. Stop believing everything anyone tells you.

I'll have you know I'm not gullible, I said. I looked up gullible in the dictionary like you told me to do, and it did not have my picture.

The God Barge and the Kid Named .45

For those of you who've been stuck in front of a screen waiting to get your bunions fixed by Obamacare, you might have missed a couple of news stories.

I'm not talking about the Mary Syndrome covered in the online news website, The Daily Beast, based on a data set of 7870 teen women followed for 14 years, that .5 percent of the 5340 who became pregnant during the study, or 45 of them, reported they were still virgins at the time of their pregnancy.

I'm not even talking about Justin Bieber's retirement.

I'm talking about two local news stories, one of which put Tillamook County in the national news, the missionary barge and the kid named .45.

Ed and Linda Ebel and their ten children and who knows who else have been building a barge at the Old Mill Marina property, or perhaps anchored in the water next to the Old Mill Marina. The details get a little fuzzy. The barge has been under construction for several months. It's now forty feet wide and eighty feet long. Hard to see it was hard to see. Apparently no Oregon State or Tillamook County official noticed a 3200 sq. ft. houseboat with twelve people living on it sitting in the middle of Tillamook Bay.

When one patient local executive told them they were violating a half-dozen regs, spanning three levels of government and the Coast Guard, the Ebels volunteered to open an espresso restaurant on the barge.

The executive surmised the couple didn't entirely understand the situation. The Coast Guard told them they couldn't take the barge across the bar. It was too wide and unstable. It would break up in the sea. They countered with the argument, the Lord would protect them since they were going to Alaska as missionaries to save fishers' souls. Good argument. I know some fishers whose souls could use some help.

The Headlight Herald reported the Ebels were stuck. I don't think so. If anyone's stuck, it's we tax payers. I doubt the Ebels have the resources to disassemble and dispose of the barge, which, as of this writing, is still growing.

But the story that put us in the national spotlight is the couple who named their child a number. Actually it wasn't a whole number. It was a fraction, 45/100ths of an inch, or .45 for short. I think they thought people would associate the baby's "name" with a well-known weapon.

It's a mystery to me why parents would want anyone who met their son for the first time to associate the child with a firearm. He could rule out a career in law enforcement, which is looking for stability in candidates. Drill instructors in the Marines would have a field day with him. He'd probably get some sympathy from a boy named Sue.

I don't know why they limited themselves to a fraction. Why not a symbol? I think Prince was named a symbol at one time. When I couldn't settle on a major in college I think my father thought my name should have been ?. They could have named him @. It would protect his domain if he ever wanted to register as an internet business.

How about #? (Just the first symbol.) He would be popular on tweets. $ probably wouldn't work if he wanted to become a monk.

You have to be licensed to drive a car. I've often thought new parents should have to take an exam and be licensed to get a kid, which is much more important than an automobile, even if it was electric. I know I should have.

A manual. When they got their kid, these parents should have been given a bad word manual to tell them how to treat a human being.

Time Is Running Out

Imagine someone told you that you only had one year left to live. How would that change your life? A death watch. Tick tock. Tick tock. The seconds left in your life are slipping away. No, I'm not being morbid. Now you can buy Tikker, a watch that counts down the number of years, months, days, hours, minutes, and yes, seconds, until you die, so you can watch on a large, dot-matrix display as the seconds you have left on Earth disappear down a black hole.

No, this isn't a Twilight Zone plot. Fredrik Colting, a 37-year-old Swedish gravedigger, says he invented the gadget he calls Tikker, the happiness watch. It's his belief that watching your life slip away will remind you to savor what you have left. Every time you look down at your watch, you will be motivated to make the right choices. While death is nonnegotiable, Fredrik says, apparently a card-carrying philosopher, life isn't. The good news is that life is what you make of it. No, don't help. I can guess the bad news.

All we have to do is learn how to cherish the time and the life that we have been given, to honor it, suck the marrow from it, seize the day, gather ye rosebuds, follow your dream or any other cliché. And the best way to do this is to realize that the time passing will never come again unless you're Buddhist (they get do-overs) and to make the right choices. Or as Steve Jobs said, the most precious resource we all have is time. Did I mention Steve Jobs is still dead?

To set up the Tikker, users fill out a questionnaire that asks about medical history, family illnesses, whether they drink or smoke, how much they weigh and whether they exercise. Tikker uses an algorithm like the one used by the federal government to figure a person's life expectancy. The user then deducts his or her current age from the results and the life countdown can begin.

Fredrik wanted some sort of reminder to not sweat the small stuff and reach for what matters. He figured imminent death was the best motivator there is.

As it turns out, there is some evidence for his point of view. One study showed that thinking about death makes you savor life more. And a 2011 study has shown that thinking about death makes you more generous, more likely to donate your blood.

But that's not the whole story. Other research suggests the effect can be chilling, a sort of incessant grim reaper reminding you that time is running out. Thinking about our own mortality can bring out the worst in us, makes us xenophobic, makes us want, if we're going to die, to do it with our own kind and so we disparage those who are different, discriminate against handicapped, other races, religions, etc. So whether Tikker will make you happy or a xenophobic serial killer is still unknown.

There is one small problem with Tikker. Okay, let's say because you bought the watch and because your frequent glances at it you do quit your job evicting underwater homeowners and get a job with Greenpeace saving whales. The problem is you're still wearing Tikker and it's still ticking. Right now the death rate is still holding steady at about 100%. The manufacturer of Tikker is like the manufacturers of collectibles who scream at you from whatever screen you're staring at, collect the entire set!

But they don't ever address the next question. Okay, I changed jobs. I've collected the entire set.

Now what?

The Essay That Changed the World

One time there was a guy who taught school a little, observed birds while picking huckleberries, had a few friends who paid his bills. He had a girlfriend once. It didn't work out. One woman proposed to him later in life. He turned her down. Since he refused to pay his taxes, you could call him a deadbeat. He died of a cold at forty-four. Not the sort of guy you would want your son to grow into.

Oh, yeah, he wrote a little.

He wrote an essay once, you know, where you give your opinion about this or that. Short of scripture, his essay has affected more people than any other piece of writing on the Earth. It inspired resistance to the McCarthy House Un-American Activities Committee hearings, opposition to the Vietnam War and every antiwar movement since. It convinced Gandhi to take India away from the British Empire, the most powerful on earth. It inspired Nelson Mandela to fight apartheid in South Africa.

His opinion piece can claim much credit for the Arab Spring, the slow increase of personal freedom in China, and the nascent blooms of democracy around the globe.

And it influenced Martin Luther King Jr, to initiate the civil rights movement.

That piece of writing doesn't ask you to take up arms. It asks you to disobey bad law. And it asks you to be civil about it. No gunfire, please.

What's ironic is it's a terrible essay. It's longish at 9500 words. It's contradictory, example, "It is truly enough said that a corporation has no conscience; but a corporation of conscientious men is a corporation *with* a conscience."

Sometimes turgid, “Only *his* vote can hasten the abolition of slavery who asserts his own freedom by his vote.”

Cynical, “Merchants and farmers here are more interested in commerce and agriculture than they are in humanity.”

Whiny, “There is but little virtue in the action of masses of men.”

Sometimes it wanders, occasionally dropping in to tell a story totally beside the point about a pleasant night spent in jail.

Sometimes it sounds like boilerplate for the Tea Party, “That government is best which governs least. That government is best which governs not at all.”

But then there is the heart of the essay, the heart Gandhi, Mandela and King, and others found and made their heart: “If it requires you to be the agent of injustice to another, then, I say, break the law.”

And “All men recognize the right of revolution; that is, the right to refuse allegiance to, and to resist, the government.”

And, “Let your life be a counter friction to stop the machine.”

“Any man more right than his neighbors constitutes a majority of one.”

“There will never be a really free and enlightened State until the State comes to recognize the individual as a higher and independent power.”

And finally this, “Under a government which imprisons any unjustly, the true place for a just man is also a prison.”

This essay will give you moral weight if you refuse to pay the new Tillamook Tourism and Lodging Tax and Sheriff Andy Long invites you stay in the Tillamook County Jail. You’ll be in good company. I understand the girl band Pussy Riot was recently released from their Russian prison for their civil disobedience.

Of course, Mandela spent twenty-seven years in jail and King and Gandhi paid with their lives. No one said civil disobedience doesn't come without a cost.

The gay, vegetarian birder who wrote the essay was Henry David Thoreau. It's called "Civil Disobedience." Monday we celebrated one of its results.

We here at the Notes-From-The-Coast R&D Department do the heavy lifting so you don't have to. You should know about this essay. An American wrote it and it changed the world.

It still is.

Snowden.

Water, Water Everywhere

Water.

A few months ago as I was perusing the front page of The Headlight Herald, I saw three of the headlines were about water, Bayocean, a town the ocean finally took by 1952, an 83-mph rainstorm during which I personally lost a shingle, and on Garibaldi's waterfront, a fish-filleting story. According to the World Health Organization, about 17 percent of the world's population doesn't have access to clean water -- that's nearly one billion people. They should move here. We've got plenty.

Of the four elements the ancients claimed made up the universe, air, earth, fire, and water, between the eight or so rivers on one side and the ocean on the other, between the devil and the deep blue sea, our element is water in this county. We are water people here. Flooding is a fact of life in Tillamook County.

Only 3 percent of the world's water supply is fresh water, and 77 percent of that is frozen. According to National Geographic, of the 23 percent that is not frozen, only a half a percent is available to supply every plant, animal and person on Earth with all the water they need to survive. You might remind yourself of this fact the next time Hwy 101 is closed because the Wilson River is over its banks again.

You can get drunk on water. Symptoms of water intoxication actually look a lot like the symptoms of alcohol intoxication, including nausea, altered mental state, and vomiting and can also be caused by bulimia or diarrhea. (This is the second time in a month I've managed a valid use of the word diarrhea in a column.)

Water intoxication causes an electrolyte imbalance that affects concentrations of salt and leads to a condition called hyponatremia, causing massive cell damage. Brain cells are constrained by the skull and can end up bursting with the pressure of the water they are taking in. The next time someone grabs the sides of the head and says you're making my brain explode, like my wife does occasionally, you might ask, how much water have you been drinking.

Sports drinks can prevent this condition by providing electrolytes, or if you're watching your budget, a glass of water with a pinch of salt and a squeeze of citrus will do the same job.

The exact amount of water intake that can lead to water intoxication is unknown and varies with each individual. Other symptoms include headaches, muscle weakness and convulsions. The condition is quite rare in the general population, but in distance athletics, it's a known risk and is often avoided by drinking sports drinks instead of water during training and events.

On January 12, 2007, radio station KDND conducted a water-drinking contest, "Hold Your Wee for a Wii" in which they promised a Wii video game system as first prize for the contestant able to hold the most water. A listener named Jennifer Strange, 28, died of water intoxication hours after taking part in the contest. The Morning Rave DJ's were fired and the station went out of business. The conclusion is obvious. Drinking too much water can be dangerous to your career.

I worry about you. Don't eat or drink more than your mother wants you to. Don't drive through floodwaters on Hwy 101. I want all of you back here next week. I want you to take care of yourselves. You and your significant other? I want you two to, too.

(Notice the three tu's in a row in the previous sentence, and it is impossible to write the previous clause grammatically correct.)

Actually, anyone who takes part in an eating or drinking contest is fodder for the Darwin Awards and doesn't belong in the (alert: water allusion) gene pool.

Baby, Baby, Baby

Whoever coined the phrase, like taking candy from a baby, must have been, one, pretty darn hungry to eat a piece of candy a baby has been gumming, and, two, if your only concern is it would be easy to steal candy from a baby because when it starts crying and the parents turn around to see what is the matter and you're holding a piece of slobbered baby candy behind your back safe in the knowledge your crime will remain hidden because the baby can't tell on you, you've got bigger problems than hunger, because you're a psychopath.

You can't listen to almost any popular song without hearing that word. Baby, not psychopath. It's an unknown fact it's the most common descriptor of your special loved one.

Well, not exactly. What we're doing when we use that word is we're describing ourselves.

We're telling our most loved one what we feel for them is past language and can only be compared to what we feel when we see a baby. And not just any baby. The baby we once were.

Assuming you're not a psychopath, whenever you see a baby, you experience an emotion that is an amalgam of joy at the possibilities for this baby and wistful regret when you compare what your baby has turned out to be, best summarized by the expression, what happened to me, I had such promise.

When you call someone baby, you're telling them you love them the way you love the baby you once were.

And you can bet your baby booties (my parents had my baby booties bronzed, it was a thing last century) the baby you once were is still alive and well but jaded and buried beneath experience.

A few years back I experienced a great pain, and when I say great, I mean it was a nine on the Sphincter Scale. And it went on for a month. I'd used up all my coping mechanisms. I was helpless.

When the pain finally abated, I was hungry. The thing is, I wanted Jell-O.

I have not intentionally eaten Jell-O since I was a teen unless some relative insisted I have that salad popular during the holidays made of Jell-O, Cool Whip, marshmallows, canned fruit cocktail retrieved from a fallout shelter, and Vaseline.

All I ate was Jell-O. Strawberry. Lime would have been way to extreme in my condition.

You've probably heard the phrase, the finest tastes are cultivated. I spent a lot of my life developing cultivated tastes. When I say cultivated, I mean acquired. When I say acquired, I mean bad.

Take dry red wine. Dry means tastes bad. You have to practice to cultivate a taste for dry red wine. If you had never drunk any and someone gave you some pinot noir, your inner baby would say, ew, this tastes bad. Your inner baby wouldn't like it, nor would it like bittersweet chocolate, single malt scotch, nor black coffee. Besides, giving a baby single malt scotch is a waste of good scotch. You can get the same effect with cheap vodka.

Babies like comfort food. Mac and cheese. That's what comfort food is, food for your inner baby.

For over a year I could not enjoy all those cultivated tastes I had spent a lifetime acquiring. They had been stripped away by pain. I was a baby again. All I wanted was comfort food.

I hate comfort food. Comfort food is for people who are stuck in the baby phase. They'll never enjoy a jalapeño nor a fine cigar.

You can't get a baby to try a jalapeño more than once, but trust me, it's hilarious.

A baby with a cigar? Even The Little Rascals knew that was funny.

Sometimes I crack myself up.

XXX...

Contrary to the reports you might have heard, I'm pretty normal. I write about what's affecting my life, figuring it's affecting yours.

We have Movienight. We invite some friends over. They bring food. They have a glass of wine, catch up since the last Movienight, eat, and watch a movie.

Our job is to pick a movie, and I'll tell you, it's not easy and it's getting harder all the time.

I was talking to one of my many fans and told him what I was worrying about. He said he monitors what's on his TV pretty closely, but one day be was watching what he thought was a mainstream movie and his five-year-old was playing with his train set and glanced at the TV. He said his boy's eyes locked on the screen, a caboose fell out of his hands, and like a zombie he started walking towards the monitor where a man and a woman were doing the naked people dance.

I don't know who coined the phase, porn has gone mainstream, but I'm not ready, even though I laugh when I hear a standup comparing his last date to a hot dog chasing a doughnut through the Hwy 26 Tunnel.

I read a food article describing the blush on the peaches as food porn. See, you just lost me. When I eat a peach, I want to just think, peach. What that writer was doing was confusing orifices.

I've wasted a lot of my life thinking about an orifice, but usually just one at a time and not while I'm eating. Well, actually, that's not true. We here at Notes tell the truth if it works. I've thought about that orifice while I was eating, running, strolling, contemplating the ocean and filling out tax forms.

Recently I've heard porn used to describe vegetables, baked goods, candy, alcohol, new cars, clothing, jewelry, high heels, and revenge. I have no idea what that last one is.

When naked people do their dance it stands for commitment, or it used to. It means dance with me and we'll raise the kids together. We'll help each other when we get sick. When we get old. It is the basis for no less than civilization. You have people dancing with each other willy-nilly without it meaning anything, and it's chaos. It would remind you of my basement.

I sound like my father or would have if we had ever talked of these things, which we didn't because, one, we were Texas males, and two, he couldn't have imagined today's porn even if I could have described it, which I would never have done because we didn't talk of such things.

My wife and I were watching what was billed as a mainstream movie and here comes this explicit sex scene. I paused the movie and told her, I couldn't have seen this much when I was a teen assuming I had the money it cost to get in.

I guess not everyone shares my discomfort. I was in a movie theater once and overheard an old woman commenting to a young woman about a particularly athletic scene, "Did that. Did that one. Did that one upside down."

I seem to be talking around the issue. Traditionally, taboos have guarded our orifices, and who was allowed in them. The bind comes when we change the role of the orifice from the entrance to the soul, to entertainment.

The naked people dance increases our respiration and heart rate. What causes the discomfort is we're not used to thinking of our children or parents, or often, friends, as sexual beings. Nor they us. The bind comes when taking the private naked people dance and making it public. In our house. In our group.

A documentary on papermaking might be a safe bet for Movienight.

How to Be a Hero

Listen, Spike, if you were born in the Northwest, I know who your hero was – Paul Bunyan, the giant, he-man logger, with his blue ox, suspenders and cork boots. My folk hero in Texas was Pecos Bill, who could rope and ride a tornado. Better known, though, was his human incarnation, Marion Morrison, the rugged, he-man cowboy with his high-heeled boots to keep his feet in his stirrups during a stampede. You probably know him by his acting name, John Wayne.

Yessir, pardner, I grew up riding horses and if you didn't I figured there was something wrong with you like you were either handicapped or from New York. My heritage was injected into my psyche like an antidefeatist antibiotic, the attitude of most Americans – if I put my mind to it, I can do anything.

Sorry, women, our culture has been remiss about female heroes. It's not that you don't have them, Abigail Adams, Harriett Tubman, Nancy Pelosi and Hillary Clinton. Don't roll your eyes at me. I can't help it if our culture has taught you to be so subservient, that you believe your place is barefoot and pregnant and in the kitchen, to the point you dislike the two strongest women in politics today. I also can't help it they're Democrats. So, go find a strong female Republican to support. You'll have to find your own way.

Like I did.

My wife Joani's core is never-give-an-inch. As you might imagine, that has plusses and minuses, especially when we disagree. She has raised a fine son. She has lived in Europe and taught young children for thirty years. She has cross-county and water skied, backpacked for years, and done a toboggan run on Mt. Hood. She is fearless. She's my hero.

And then came that day she was diagnosed with a degenerative nerve disease.

Since then, she has been, from her wheelchair, President of the Pacific City Library Board, the Thrift Shop Board, a volunteer reader for SMART, is a regular fundraiser for and has made too many contributions to Tillamook County to name.

There was nothing wrong with her. The problem was me.

While I was forming into John Wayne, ready to rope and ride a tornado to Oregon, he never said, smile when you call me a caregiver, Pilgrim.

When anyone mentioned the word caregiver, I got all clammy. You did, too, especially if you are of the male persuasion. Extra especially if you're under forty.

That's pretty funny because we all started out with a caregiver. Who do you think changed your diapers?

I had no models to show me how to be a caregiver. John Wayne, Hulk Hogan, Bruce Willis, nor Chuck Norris were caregivers. Arnold never said, Schwarzenegger is my name, caregiving is my game. Super heroes weren't caregivers. Not even Wonder Woman. At one point I even considered running away.

The Americans With Disabilities Act has been law for two and a half decades. Condensed, it states if you're not handicapped you have to park far away.

Actually, it says if you have a disability, which is the inability to perform a major life function like walking or shopping at Costco, you can't be denied services provided to the public. I urge you not to use businesses where a wheelchair can't get in. They've had twenty-four years to comply.

As I look around, I can see there is nothing special about what I'm doing. I see caregivers everywhere, teachers and nurses, of course, but many spouses and all parents.

There is no way what I say next isn't self-serving. This is for men. It takes a real man to be a caregiver.

Ultimately, this isn't Joani's story, or even mine. It's yours, because if you're lucky, that is, if you live long enough, you'll either need one or be one.

Become an Art Critic in 2 Easy Steps

For the number of people we have in Tillamook County, we've got a lot of galleries.

Okay, so you're not all that big on art. The few times you've been dragged into a gallery by friends, someone made a comment about what a piece was saying, how the artist used the elements of structure and color in a harmonious whole to comment on the humankind's effort to achieve enlightenment. Yeah, you said.

What you saw was a streak of color that reminded you of that Saturday when you spilled the paint.

And not only that, you weren't in the mood, not since you took that pottery class and your spouse told you the dog left something on your workbench.

You never got the art thing. It made you feel dumb.

Let me just say, you're not stupid.

I'm going to teach you a new phrase that will protect you while you're trying to figure out the art thing. The phrase is, it doesn't speak to me.

Step 1 - The next time someone asks what you think or don't you agree, repeat the phrase, it doesn't speak to me. Instead of people thinking you're ignorant, now they'll think you're not only wise but hard to please.

Here's what's going on with that painting. The artist isn't really thinking that much. They're feeling and who knows what they're feeling. Guess what? That's not your job. Art isn't about the artist. It's about you.

Step 2 - Figure out what you're feeling. Your feelings are your feelings and they're never wrong. You might make a mistake adding a series of numbers or installing a new faucet, but you can't make a mistake feeling. Say what you're feeling.

You're now an art critic.

What you missed is you've been both an artist and an art critic all along. Even if you've never sculpted or spread oil on canvas you've been seized by art. Anyone who has decorated a birthday cake or pinstriped a logging truck or wrote for fun or sewn a quilt or sang along with the radio has done art.

Art is when you create something. Art critic is when you step back and say, well, that sucks or when you want to stand back for a minute and admire what you've created. Time spent admiring should exceed time spent creating.

A guy named Andrei Codrescu edited a literary journal named The Exquisite Corpse. He named it that because he knows pieces of art are dead. They were alive at one time when someone was creating them. As soon as the artist, sculptor, writer, whatever, was finished, the result, people call it art, died. It's an exquisite corpse.

It can come alive again, but only with your help. When you see it or read it or hear it, it comes alive, but not out there somewhere. It comes alive inside you. It makes you feel something and so it is reborn. If not, it doesn't speak to you.

Remember, you're the critic. If it doesn't make you feel, it isn't art. If it does, it's art and if it makes you feel deeply, it's good art. If it gives you joy by making you feel maybe you might have an insight into the big questions, why are we here, what is the point to it all, it's great art.

I think you're ready to visit a gallery.

Where No One Knows Your Name

I saw the Deep Web. It creeped me out. I wasn't going to do a column on it. It's not funny and dangerous, but it's like a car wreck, hard to look away. Okay, not a Three-Stooge-eye-poke dangerous, although it looks painful when Larry does it to Curly, but real danger.

Everybody knew my name where I grew up. I couldn't get away with anything. It's not much different now where my photo is in the paper because I want fans to feel free, like two did recently, to accuse me of being a Democrat because I said the two strongest women in politics are Democrats. Also, I'm getting emails telling me what an idiot Hillary is. I wonder if I said the Three Stooges are funny they'd accuse me of being the Fourth Stooge, nyuk, nyuk.

Like I said, I wasn't going to write about the Deep Web, but NPR scooped me this morning, so now I'm playing catch up

Oops. I guess I told on myself. Well, maybe not. I'm sure there must be a Republican somewhere who listens to NPR. Probably in Oregon.

The Deep Web is most of the Internet. When you do a Google search for pickled okra, even though you get hundreds pages, you'd think that's all there is, right? Wrong. Google searches only .03% of the Internet. That doesn't mean there are 99.97 times more pickled okra recipes on the Deep Web. What does it mean then?

The Deep Web is devoted to avoiding the law. Which law? Any law. All law.

If you want, you can figure out how to access the Deep Web, but beware. If the first instructions are disable cookies, put up your firewall and don't download anything, not even a pdf, then it's a nasty part of town.

If you had $20K you didn't need and knew how to convert it to bit coin, you could eliminate an annoying columnist who might or might not be a Democrat. A County Commissioner will cost you $30K. I'm not joking, and I'm offended. To think a columnist is valued only 2/3 of a County Commissioner. White Wolves or C'thulhu are vendors of choice.

Drugs vacuumed packed four times and shipped to your house, illegal credit cards with pin's (if you shopped at Target last Christmas, perhaps your credit card) any firearm you can imagine (you're responsible for shipping tanks), items you'd like stolen, fixed sports events you can bet on, any porn imaginable and some you couldn't, and some activities I wouldn't write here, or even speak about, they're so disturbing.

There are a lot of suspect, compromised, degenerate and ultimately, monstrous human beings doing illegal things on it. As a species, Camper, we are quite a piece of work. Why aren't these people in jail?

Because no one knows their name. Once you download the browser you need to surf the Deep Web, which you probably already have in your Applications folder on your computer, you're anonymous. When you request a service, no one knows your name. You pay with bit coin, which is anonymous.

Recently the government managed to infiltrate the Deep Web somewhat. You might have read about Silk Road, an eBay-like crime shopping site. It was shut down and the owner put in jail. One down, 200 million to go.

That's what happens when no one knows our name. We behave badly. Neighborhood planners found the crime rate went down if people shared a common recreation area so everyone knows your name.

I'm going to need an awful lot of The Three Stooges to clear my head after researching the Deep Web. Make that clean.

If you of the Republican persuasion would like to send former President George W. Bush an expression of your gratitude for serving as President for eight years, go ahead. You can buy his private email on the Deep Web.

Mr. News Guy Explains Ethics

Isn't it unethical, Mr. News Guy, to demand payment to be interviewed?

Just ask the questions.

These aren't even my questions. What are ethics and how can they work for you?

The Society of Professional Journalists Code of Ethics states it is the duty of the journalist is provide a fair and comprehensive account of events and issues unless there was a car wreck with great photos.

What?

Blood helps. If there's no blood, then a kid, preferably under five. Or a puppy. A kid with a puppy? Click bait. Now you're talking journalism.

It doesn't say that.

Something close. Anyway it should if you want to stay in business.

You can't be serious.

As a heart attack. Give the average reader the choice of an analysis of controlled forest fire burns versus benign neglect and a story on puppy barking alerting a four-year-old who called 911 and saved a girl scout troop selling cookies in a burning mall and see which story runs.

But, Mr. News Guy, what about the duty of the paper to inform?

Inform this. The most popular "paper" is an online news source called The Daily Beast, as in the news is a beast and always needs feeding, previously Newsweek. Photos eat text 8 to 1, and they're celebs, criminals, dictators, sports figures, you can fill in the rest. Once they get the eyeballs they might slip in something without cleavage, like one religious sect massacring another. Guess what percentage read it?

You're painting a pretty bleak journalistic picture, Mr. News Guy. What about the Wall Street Journal? They're mainly text and serious.

Right. They're paid more than I am. What a concept, a paper for the rich.

The next question I'm supposed to ask, due to all the fame and natural sex appeal that comes with your job, how do I get a career as a newspaper columnist, also?

Forget for a minute about the big salary, the acknowledgement from the community in the form of head nods when I'm out and about and a new nonverbal sign of endearment with which I'm not familiar, the holding up a fist out front and the clasping of the elbow with the other hand, which means, I'm sure, power to you, Mr. News Guy. This calling was my destiny.

Isn't it true no one else on staff wanted it?

That's not one of the questions. How do I get me some ethics, I can hear you asking.

How do I get me some ethics?

An experienced, smart editor, comfortable walking the razor edge of danger, is invaluable in a search for ethics. I have such an editor now.

You have absolutely no shame, do you?

When it works. It also helps to have a fine eye for color. Let's say I turn in a column comparing the Thanksgiving Dinner with several of the body parts of, oh, say, Dolly Parton, with photos, and my editor turns red and says, you're fired, I know I've pushed the edge of the ethics envelope. If, instead, she just turns pale and says we are so not printing this, I know I'm closer to the mark.

Mr. News Guy, are you the definition of journalistic integrity, it says here?

Scratch that. I'm just a schmuck trying to make a living. I didn't create this world. I just comment on it.

I heard you were sent to a workshop and they had a lifeboat exercise. Your group decided to throw you out of the lifeboat even though they had plenty of food and water. Comment?

I guess they didn't like what I said. So, how old are you, twelve? Listen, sweetheart, on second thought, don't worry your pretty little head about any of this, ok? No, I shouldn't say that. You know right from wrong, don't you? Just write it.

One Thing I Didn't Count On

I've noticed the phrase one thing I didn't count on seems to be a reoccurring theme in my life.

One thing I didn't count on is how similar Abraham Lincoln and I are. We both have a good sense of humor. He used to slap his knee, laughing. He and I started out poor. I never wrote on a shovel in front of a fire or anything, although I thought that would have been so cool. And when I say poor, I don't mean I missed any meals. I had just enough to envy my best friend Jack who had better hair, skin, teeth, car and girl friend, Joyce. Jack knew I had a crush on his Chevy. Although I never told Joyce, I think she suspected.

A few examples of things I didn't count on are how little cayenne it takes to make chili inedible. How a cardboard flap is not strong enough to hold a new, boxed hot water heater at the top of a flight of stairs. An outboard motor will not go into a garage in the upright position.

If my father got overtime, we moved from poor to middle class for that week, and so I was taught to stretch my dollars. He did everything himself. If you didn't he thought it showed weakness of character. We didn't build our own furniture or anything like I'm sure the Lincoln's did, but we changed the oil in our cars and tuned them up. Lincoln would have done his own tune-ups if there had been cars. I'm sure if there hadn't been a White House, he would have thrown one together.

The problem with this line of logic is I'm not Lincoln or my father, for that matter. Neighbors can tell when I'm finished tuning up my car when they see the tow truck arrive.

When I finally graduated I didn't make a quiet entrance into the middle class. I didn't slip into the suburbs without fanfare, going to a local store and having a set of furniture delivered one afternoon. Oh, no. That would have shown weakness of character. I convinced my wife, even though I couldn't build our own furniture, we could pick up an entire houseful cheaper bidding at auction. One thing I didn't count on was the affect adrenaline and beer has on the bidding process.

Another thing I didn't count on was how being nervous affects my memory. I took Joani to meet friends. As we approached the front door I realized I couldn't remember her name. I was unperturbed, thinking, it will come to me. I just married her.

At the front door I said, I'd like you to meet my wife...

After a long pause, Joani said, Joani. I doubt Lincoln ever forgot Mary's name. Can you believe we just celebrated our 32nd anniversary? Or maybe it was our 42nd.

And then there was the laundry massacre. Even though Joani does the bills and I do the laundry, she's particular about her blouses. I had barbecued ribs coming off the grill, people arriving, and permanent press coming out of the dryer. My daughter-in-law volunteered to take the laundry.

Locking up at midnight, I was tired and so didn't think when I saw the laundry hanging near the ceiling where I'd never seen it before. My daughter-in-law had hung it on the garage door track.

One thing I didn't count on was how long it took me to understand what was happening when I punched the button. As the garage door started to close, it marched the laundry along the ceiling and pulled it off a cliff down the greasy track where it ended up crumpled in a pile on the floor.

Abraham Lincoln would have been no help since he never had a garage door opener, but one thing I could have counted on -- he would have been slapping his knee.

We're a Salad!

On March 25, 1989, Tim Berners-Lee invented the Internet, which means the Internet just had its 25th birthday. Did you get a card?

There could not have been a random act fraught with more unforeseen consequences since Mrs. O'Leary's cow torched Chicago. Just think how much worse off you'd be without the Internet. You wouldn't have those raspberry drops to help you lose weight, you couldn't make $100K helping a Somalian prince get his father's gold out of the country, and you wouldn't have an endless supply of hilarious cartoons mocking the things you cherish. If you wanted to steal someone's identity, you'd have to get in your car and drive to their house.

On the other hand, the Internet has fractured our center by burying us with choices. I now understand the Yeats poem, things fall apart; the centre cannot hold.

The center hasn't held, or more accurately, the center is changing.

For thousands of years we've had a center. It was religion, poems, songs, dances, big buildings like temples, and the belief in The Lone Ranger. We all knew the words to the songs. We knew the steps to the dances. We gathered at the Walmart. We shouted hi ho, Silver, away.

As late as a century ago, even before I was born, people used to gather around a radio as big as a freezer and warm themselves in the glow of the radio tubes and listen to The Lone Ranger. Quite frankly, I thought he was weird even then.

Later we gathered around the television to watch The Lone Ranger. I'll give Kimosabe legs.

Even today we could gather around a movie to watch Johnny Depp as Tonto making fun of The Lone Ranger.

With the Internet we don't know where the center is anymore. We're like little kids used to a wood stove on a cold morning, and suddenly we're in a new house with central heating. After our mother gets us up, we wander around like short zombies in pajamas looking for something warm.

We used to describe our center as a melting pot. The problem with a melting pot is everything becomes the same. You can get in trouble using the wrong metaphor.

Our center was never a melting pot. We were never all the same. We were from Europe and China and Mexico and Africa. We were Jews and Christians and Moslems. We were straight and gay. We were a salad.

With a salad you can still identify the vegetables, and they taste good together. (I'm resisting the urge to identify a race or gender with a vegetable.)

Recently we have watched movies on Amazon, House of Cards on Netflix and the new Seinfeld on comediansincarsgettingcoffee.com. See? No center.

Oh, sure, you're going to post what you re watching. You'll check your screens to read what everyone else is watching. God forbid you should actually speak to someone. About the only events everyone watches together as it's happening anymore is the Superbowl commercials and the Oscars.

There are so many options now. There are hundreds of YouTube "shows" with a million viewers. The cool thing is, someone else isn't making the artistic decisions for us. We don't have to watch what we're given. We're creating our new center ourselves.

We watched something recently called Submissions Only on YouTube. It was funny and sweet and amateurish. It was a delight. You can see actors who aren't ready for prime time and the ones with real talent who will be the stars of tomorrow like Jared Gertner. All of the races and the four genders were represented, or maybe six. The center is more complicated now. It was so refreshing. It was a salad.

Hm. I think I'll just have the salad.

What Was the Question?

A recent issue of the HH reported a position taken by Tillamook County Commissioners on dispensing medical marijuana. Their position was no. The subheadline rhetorical question posed by Commissioner Baertlein was, what kind of message would we be sending to our children.

It was a good question, but the logic was hard to follow. Commissioner Baertlein doesn't want a medical marijuana dispensary next to a school because of the children, I suppose. Does he propose to locate the dispensary somewhere in Tillamook County where there are no children? I wasn't aware Tillamook County had children-free zones?

I digress. I decided to do research to find out if medical marijuana dispensaries went in next to schools or anywhere, for that matter, what message would we be sending.

In an effort to uphold the highest tradition of HH journalistic excellence, this columnist went "underground" to gather evidence to answer that question. I probably should have notified my editor, but since I don't really have an editor right now, I was good to go.

I filled out my expenses reimbursement form. I didn't see a blank for medical marijuana. Also, I wasn't clear as to the difference between medical marijuana and the regular kind. If there isn't a difference, are patients given a handout instructing them, this marijuana is for medicinal use? Do not attempt to have "fun" with it?

To avoid any confusion, we'll just call it "product."

The first thing I needed to do was acquire some "product." Fortunately I had a "source" in the form of a friend. For the purpose of this account we'll just call him "Bill Wadsworth."

"Bill" came right over when I told him what I needed to do. He brought some "product."

My next-door neighbor just happened to stop by. For the purpose of this article we'll just call him "Gary Parrett."

That looks like some mighty fine "product," "Gary" said.

Yes, it does, I responded, but "Gary," this is only for medicinal use. I'm not supposed to enjoy it.

"Gary" looked confused.

Also, "Gary," it's been so long since I tested any "product," I don't remember exactly how it's done. The last time I tested "product" was The Sixties, which really didn't occur until the seventies. In any case I don't remember a lot about the Sixties, whenever they took place, which I'm told is good evidence I was there. It seems we used something shaped like a recorder to test "product."

Oh, "Gary," said, you mean a (for the purpose of this article we'll call "Gary's" device a "bing") a "bing?"

Right, I said. A "bing."

I've got a "bing," "Gary" said. Or I used to, if I can remember where I put it. "Gary" came back with the "bing." We both stared at it.

It looks kind of complicated, "Gary."

I think your thumb goes here and this finger goes here, "Gary" said.(After a couple of testing sessions, I had trouble remembering which words go "in" quotation marks.)

My wife put her foot down. Your "research" is hurting my ears. You've got the stereo volume set on nine. And if you're going to continue to use the "bing," she said, we're going to have to allot more in the budget for snack foods. You ate everything in the house.

I'm through testing and have completed phase one of my research, I told my wife. I answered Commissioner Baertlein's question, but as is often the case, when you answer one question, it just generates more questions.

In phase two of my research, I used my "computer." Here is what I found. Since 1700 college students die each year from alcohol abuse, and since the total number of alcohol-induced deaths for 2012 was 25,692, and since you can buy alcohol in practically any neighborhood store regardless of a school's location and since according to drugwarfacts.org, there has never been recorded a death with marijuana as the cause, I, too, have a question.

What is the message we're sending to our children now?

I Don't Believe in Objects

My father had a job driving a streetcar. He had to arrive at an intersection within a minute or two. That would be different than now when managers are pretty happy if their employees arrive at work within an hour or two.

He had to own an accurate watch. It was a pocket watch. You can see them in museums. They didn't tell the barometric pressure, elevation, direction, your heart rate, or produce an image of a loved one, live, you could tell to pick up some toilet paper on the way home. They just told the time.

It was a mechanical watch, meaning it had little gears inside and a knurled knob at the top you had to wind or it wouldn't work. The numbers didn't blink. They were painted inky black on a white face.

My father's watch was a 21-jewel Hamilton Railroad watch. The jewels were rubies and other rare stones of extreme hardness. They were not for decoration. You couldn't even see them unless you took the back off the watch. They were used for pivot points for the gears.

His watch said quality, which is one of those words you understand less after looking it up. You know it, though, when you're in its presence, even if you're only four years old. Then quality was heavy. Now it's light.

Occasionally he would let me hold it. I had to be in his lap. I liked the holding of his watch. I liked the being in his lap. I remember it in detail, turning it over in my little hands, the polished slick feel of it, eighteen carat gold. It was heavy.

There was a market for high-quality watches even before my father's time. Two telegraph operators started a business selling them. Their names were Roebuck and Sears.

His railroad watch, for him, cost a lot. If something had happened to my father's watch, it would have been a family tragedy, for if he couldn't have replaced it, he would have been fired.

There is a movie about such a tragedy. It is short, sixty minutes or so, but it is on the best movie list of every movie critic who has ever written, including Roger Ebert's. It's about what happens when objects become such a part of us we'll turn over our morality for them. In the movie it wasn't a watch. It was a bicycle. The movie is The Bicycle Thief.

I don't believe in objects. My wife would say I don't believe in cleaning them, either. A large part of my life has been a battle against my objects. You become attached to an object and they break, break your heart, or worse, you try to give them to your kids and they don't want them.

The worst are books, which took over one room and sent feelers into the living room, but I'm winning because I'm ruthless. (Usually I have lots of ruth.) I got rid of my books. I use our public library.

I threw my degrees away. We have too many windows so we have a lack of wall space. What, I'm going to hang my degrees in the bathroom like it's a small office? My wife thinks it already is. With some drama, I dropped my framed degrees into the garbage can. My wife gasped, as if I had self-administered brain surgery and had thrown away a chunk of my gray matter.

Besides, as anyone who has ever had to clear objects out of a dead parent's house can tell you, you don't own your objects. You're just renting them. So when you die, you're taking your pool table with you?

Even worse than wasting love on an object is treating a person like one.

Let's Put on a Play!

In a bakery recently I noticed for the first time age spots on the back of my hands. I said something about them and the young woman behind the counter said, oh, they're angel kisses. Well, I said, it looks like the angels have slobbered a map of Indonesia on me.

One of my friends commented, your columns are trending. You mean I'm more popular than ever. No, they're turning macabre. People getting sick, getting old and dying. You're beginning to sound like a list of side effects of prescription drugs, dizziness, deterioration, coma and death.

That's not true. I'm upbeat. I'm hilarious. People read me to get a lift to their day. I make people laugh.

Mickey Rooney died. If you're in the half of my readers who will say, who, try to imagine rolling into one, Robin Williams, Jack Black, Billy Crystal and Will Farrell. If you're in the other half, he was just Rooney. I've been watching Rooney on the screen since I've been watching screens.

Rooney would have said, I'm a small actor, 5'2" to be exact.

That was the only thing about him that was small. He appeared in more American movies than anyone, 241. He made and lost and made and lost fortunes. He got to sing with Judy Garland. He was married eight times, once to Ava Gardner (Way to go, Mickey. If you say who, you need to google her.) His acting career lasted more than ninety, that's a nine and a zero, years.

Rooney was ebullient. He didn't apologize for looking on the bright side. Today if we find the IRS is going to take the farm, I'd resort to the nihilistic solution from Animal House. Road trip!

In Rooney's movies, he said, let's put on a play!

You can see him in the dozens of movies he made as a frustrated teen wanting to smooch Judy Garland, but if you want to reacquaint yourself with his natural talent, I recommend A Midsummer's Night's Dream with Rooney as the irrepressible sprite, Puck, along with James Cagney, Merle Oberon, Dick Powell and Joe E. Brown. Rooney will make you smile at a performance that convinces you he just might be a sprite for real.

Last year he made an appearance in one of my columns. I was writing about how in addition to reading my son Josh bedtime stories, we frequently did vaudeville routines. Doctor, I have a cough. Ever had it before? Yes. Well, you've got it again. Doctor, it hurts when I do that. Don't do that.

Josh knew about Rooney and his vaudeville routines, so when Sugar Babies, a vaudeville review starring Rooney and Ann Miller came to town, Joani and I took Josh. Rooney is walking among the audience in overalls doing a routine as a handyman banging on things while Ann Miller is trying to sing on stage. They send zingers back and forth.

Since Sugar Babies is a bit bawdy, Rooney sees Josh, the only seven-year-old in the audience, second row, aisle seat. The spotlight is following Rooney as he moves about, walks up and stands beside Josh. It widens to take in just the two of them, Rooney holding out his hand, Josh putting his hand in Rooney's hand, illuminating them in the darkness as Rooney goes on with the show.

Why did he do that? Because he was telling Josh, no matter what we say in this skit, I'm taking care of you. What kind of man will stoop to help, understands the power of touch, that it's personal, it's acceptance, that it's a wordless blessing. A great man does.

But then Josh is used to great men. He also shook hands with the President of the United States.

I don't seem to have as much energy as I used to.

Did I mention Josh just turned forty?

Taking Out the Garbage is Illogical

Did you hear that guy on the radio tell the temperature of a recently discovered dwarf planet?

Dwarf isn't politically correct. You're supposed to say little planet. How do they know?

Logic. You know in the summertime you can look way down the highway and see those wavy lines off in the distance? Deductive logic tells you heat is radiating off the asphalt?

Not on the coast.

Uh, right. Somewhere there's heat. If you calibrated those wavy lines using inductive logic, which uses measurements, you could tell the temperature of the road.

Did you put out the garbage?

I forgot. Did you hear that guy on the radio telling how the dinosaurs were wiped out?

They froze.

No, they baked.

No, they didn't. They froze. This meteor hit the earth and sent a bunch of dust into the air, which blocked the sun's warmth and froze the dinosaurs.

That's what I'm trying to tell you, there's this new theory. They baked. When that meteor hit, it went twenty miles into the earth's crust. The heat from the impact converted rock into gas and shot it into space. The gasified rock cooled into little glass beads the size of sand. Some of them hit the moon. Some, Mars. Most were pulled back to earth by gravity. When those glass beads hit earth's atmosphere, each one created just a little bit of heat, like the astronauts experience when coming back to earth. That's why the heat shield on the capsule. There were so many of them, as they reentered, they raised the temperature of the atmosphere to 1200 degrees. All the dinosaurs cooked in about two hours.

So nothing survived?

No, they're not saying that. If you had been below ground, only three inches or so, or a crocodile in several inches of mud, you would have been fine. Sixty-six million years ago this event laid down a layer of those glass beads everywhere on our planet. Below the layer, lots of dinosaur fossils. Above, none.

Is that where we come in?

Right. The reason we became dominant was before the asteroid we were tiny. After everything on the surface was toast, we'd be the biggest dog on the block.

What were we?

An hypothetical placental mammal.

Hypothetical?

Because scientists use deductive logic to project backwards based on versions we have fossil records for.

Why aren't there fossils for it?

They didn't say, but you have to have faith in the logic. You use it all the time. Your computer runs on it. They're called algorithms.

Faith? In my computer? That's your argument? Do you not remember how often my computer crashes?

They say we would have had black, beady eyes, fleshy ears and nose and a pale, pink underbelly. Our teeth could both tear meat and grind plants. We were omnivores. Shrews.

You did not just call me a shrew.

Uh, no, I didn't.

I'm incensed. I'm used to being told I came from a knuckle-dragging ape. Now I'm told I was a shrew? I wasn't even a monkey? I was a rat?!

I don't think they meant it the way you're taking it. The meteor was a good thing. Without it we would be still living in the topsoil.

You would. I'd be a tunnel-dwelling minx who would pounce on you the second you stuck up your tiny, beady-eyed little head.

Probably.

I've never been so insulted in my life. I'm so not going to believe that.

But that's illogical. You have to believe it. It's science.

No, it's perfectly logical not to believe it because every theory before has been wrong. The earth is flat. No, it isn't. It's round and the center of the universe. No, the sun is the center of the universe. No, the sun is a minor star at the edge of the Milky Way. I'm not going to believe that theory until you take out the garbage. You know what theory I'd like to believe in? A universe where you take out the garbage. But that's illogical.

Dirty Words

I heard an interview of an author who wrote a book called The F Word. He said we don't cuss enough. He must be watching different movies.

The dead comedian George Carlin performed a routine called, the 7 Dirty Words. My father had a lot more than seven if he heard me say he would have locked me in the stocks he installed in the back yard when he realized one day he would have a teenage male living in his house.

Dirty words are either based on religion or bodily functions. Any cussing that refers to a deity is called profanity. Wishing you to an uncomfortably warm place for a long time we'll call the D word to the H word. There are substitutes for the D word, like darn and drat, which, informatively, is the shortened version for may God rot you in the H word.

All the rest came from the Anglo-Saxons, the original party animals whose idea of a good time when they weren't jumping in their ships and invading their neighbors, lopping off a limb or two, was to talk about bowel movements and reproduction. Since eloquence wasn't their long suit, they used a lot of single-syllable, four-letter words you can still hear today on playgrounds and TV.

I must have been out of the country when butt and boobs became acceptable. When I tried to explain to my students those words were not appropriate for the classroom, they were sincerely puzzled and asked, but why not, Mr. Moore?

I explained I was raised in the South and Southerners didn't say such things. In fact, at one time the word "leg" was unacceptable. I explained as if I were describing bizarre social customs of an alien group on another continent, Southern women sewed pantaloons or leggings to be attached to piano legs lest a young suitor coming to call would glance at the naked piano leg while their daughter was playing and have an impure thought.

When I tried to get back to the lesson, they begged, please, Mr. Moore, tell us more of the mating habits of Southerners.

Okay, but just one more for now. Woman was a dirty word. Really, their eyes wide with amazement? Then what did they call them? Ladies, I replied. Woman was used to refer to females of low moral character. Actually, it was more a label of wealth. If you were poor, you were a woman, rich, a lady.

The girls flopped their hands over to boys near them, batted their eyelashes and said, I'm a lay-dee, except for Ursala, of course, who said in a guttural voice, H word, I'll always be a wo-man.

The reason you're not supposed to use dirty words frequently is they lose their power. If you hit your finger with a hammer and you're using the D word all the time, you get no satisfaction. It's an unknown fact the healing power of the D word is reduced the more it's used.

Dirty words are used not only by sailors, as I was taught, or because the speaker lacks vocabulary, since educated people without sail boats sometimes use them, as did my mother. Actually, my mother didn't use the D word. She said dang. However, she informed us three dangs equaled the D word, and it was my sisters' and my responsibility to keep track. I heard one dang, I'd whisper to my sister. How many did you hear? Two. I didn't hear the second one. I'm telling you I heard two, so you better watch out.

When I was ten I wanted to say the F word, but I was afraid to. I rode my bicycle up to the power station by our house, got off and looked around. I took a deep breath and shouted, "Fart!"

Later my friend Buddy Collins informed me there was another F word.

I Hereby Propose to the Constitution

Retired Justice of the Supreme Court John Paul Stevens has in a recent book proposed six amendments to the Constitution of the United States.

I know a whiskey sour from an old fashioned. I don't see why I have to pass some arbitrary bar exam. I don't know why a respected local columnist can't propose a few amendments.

An amendment to the Constitution should require you, when you ask me how I'm doin', to maintain eye contact for three minutes while I tell you.

Store clerks who shrug should be legally required to wear around their neck a sign that says, I Have No Idea Why I Was Hired.

You want the dessert? Order the dessert. Eat it and shut up about it. The Constitution should require wait staff for people who spend half the dinner talking about their latest diet and then order dessert and say, oh, I'm going to be so very bad, to snatch the dessert away before it's tasted and seat them in the corner facing the wall wearing a dunce hat.

I would like to see as a part of the Constitution an immediate cause for a forfeit if any athlete or coach crosses himself, uses the term God, expresses a religious opinion, or prays for divine intervention for the outcome of a sporting event. Besides, everyone knows God is a Packers fan.

When you've invited people to your party and while watching you serve they give you "helpful" suggestions how to save the planet, they should be confined to another room and made to listen to Ralph Nader's 2000 Presidential campaign stump speeches.

It should be legally required for anyone who uses the term software or operating system at a party to be confined to the same room.

The Constitution should require you as the host of your party to anyone who says to make a long story short, which means you're going to get the long version, to say, "Stop. I know someone who wants the long version." Then take them to the Ralph Nader room.

An amendment should require the issuing of a citation to anyone who slows down when they see a police car.

Federal law should require the issuance of a citation to any driver who does not make a driver in the next lane with a blinker on feel welcome to cut in front.

No matter where your children live, they should be legally required at least four times a year to bring your grandchildren to your house and let you give them anything they want to eat. Your children should have to repeat to their children the words yes, grandma and grandpa are great.

The Constitution should require the cancelation of cable service to anyone who invites you to their house and continues to watch TV.

Unless you're waiting for an organ transplant, constitutional law should require cell phones turned off when you go to visit.

The Constitution should require vegetarians and Republicans to listen to my side while nodding occasionally.

Federal law should require a donation of ten percent of profits to your favorite charity made by anyone who tells you how well they did in the market.

Even if I claim I believe the CIA shot Kennedy, Area 57 is an alien zoo, global warming is caused by a Martian Death Star, Mrs. Lincoln shot Mr. Lincoln, the Communists are battling the KKK for world domination, the meaning of life is we are an experiment run by teen galactic science students, which makes more sense than what I'm told, that I'm right and my spouse Joani is wrong (see Lincolns), it should be a violation of the Constitution for anyone to tell me what to think.

Or, I guess, you.

Give Me Puberty or Give Me Death

Our life is marked by boundaries, and if you're male, fistfights. There is the boundary of starting and completing school, bonding with another, getting a job, having children, and retiring and becoming a columnist. Most boundaries are happy events marked by celebrations. There are two boundaries we cross that are fraught with confusion and fear – puberty and death.

If you lived in anyplace in the world except the U.S., there would be a ceremony to help you cross the boundary between childhood and adulthood. In most countries, for females, the boundary is marked by the beginning of the first menses. In this country it's the first cell phone. She looks down and texts her best friend, I'm a woman.

For males, it's more confusing. You no longer want to sneak a lizard into Linda Clark's lunch sack. You still want to do something to her. You just have no idea what it is. Rubbing lips is still gross and you believe will force you to give up your recently acquired membership you got from the back of a magazine in the Mixed Martial Arts Cage Fighting Association.

The Jews think puberty happens to everyone on a Saturday. Catholics assume it's your fault. Protestants blame dancing. Muslims will inform you when it happens.

If you lived 2300 years ago in Greece, you believed in a literal boundary between life and death. It was a river. You got in a boat, and Charon, a scary boatman with poor hygiene, polled you cross the Stix River for coins, usually held in your mouth or on your eyes. He gave you a brochure – Welcome to Hades!

Because we've tried to repress what it was like to be a teenager, we know almost nothing about them. Teenagers have a coded language that prevents us from understanding them. Just because you know that SWAG means cool, YOLO means you only live once, SMH means shake my head in disbelief, MOSS means chill out, and CHIRPING means griping, don't feel swag, moss and quit chirping, because smh, yolo.

As with teenagers, we know almost nothing about what a dying person perceives. Are you okay? *No, I'm not okay. Are you not paying attention? I'm dying.* Need anything? *I need everything.*

Just like teens, dying people get depressed, usually not the jump-out-the-window depressed but what-the-hell-has-happened depressed. I had so much left I wanted to do. I wanted to see how things turned out.

If you've been doing your job, you've been telling your child from the time they were toddlers babies don't come via drone from Amazon. Puberty causes them. If not, you're best bet is to get help with your teen by asking those whose job is to spend time with them daily, and as hard as it is to believe, actually like it, counselors, ministers, psychologists, and teachers who like kids.

Even though the dying are easier to understand than teens, you're best choice is hospice. Because they are in death's presence daily, they recognize death. They know when it's in the room. They'll often give us a ritual, that although it has little effect on the dying, makes us feel better, like using an eyedropper to put water in the dying's parched mouth while saying our name. Hospice angels will tell you, because even though they're dying now, they can still hear you. I have no idea how they know this. Perhaps they're tuned to a different channel.

Which is different for teens. Even though they're looking directly at you, and no matter on which channel you're broadcasting, they still can't hear you.

Writingbot vs. Verb-Drivin' Man

When an earthquake rumbled in southern California recently, Ken Schwencke of the Los Angeles Times was interviewed about a writing robot called Quakebot guided by a writing algorithm which generated a newspaper article about it within three minutes.

I know what you're thinking. Schubert, we're all so worried about your job. Is it possible for a robot to write your column?

Well, for one thing, Quakebot doesn't have a fetching headshot like I do. On the other hand it didn't charge overtime, and I'll have to admit, three minutes is a pretty quick turnaround.

But calm your racing pulse and put down that bottle of JD. I've got a pretty good algorithm myself, as I was told recently at the end of my Zumba workout.

When my editor asked, does Quakebot complain about its editor, Schwencke said no.

See, that's a key difference right there. Quakebot doesn't sound like any writer I know. A writer who doesn't complain about his editor isn't a real writer.

Oh, I guess that's the point.

My editor has much more respect for me than he would for some algorithm-generated writing robot. He welcomes criticism. If, for instance, I said my editor could use some helpful criticism because of his tendency to (deleted), he wouldn't mind at all.

Would I have a beer with Quakebot? Depends on who's buying.

Sure, I would have a drink with the little columnist wannabe. I'm not a bot bigot.

Take the subject of happiness I'm currently writing about. What would Quakebot do with that? Researchers recently tried to determine the cause of happiness. Granted, they were Liberal researchers. I mean, what Conservative researcher would waste government funds trying to find the cause of happiness? They would try to find the cause of unhappiness.

The researchers called volunteers at random on their cell phones asking them if their mind was wandering and how happy they were. The first thing I'd like to say is of course they called them on their cell phones. Who has a land line anymore?

I happened to get one of those calls, which interrupted an hour-long phone survey, assisting a high-level educational research group funded by Home Shopping Network, which interrupted a documentary I was supposed to be watching on wool dying. I was trying to keep my mind from wandering to the next selection on my Netflix queue, Attack of the Fifty-Foot Vampiress with a D-Cup.

The researcher said in his/her call, (it's becoming more and more difficult to tell gender over the phone and I don't know how to talk to them unless I know their gender. Her, his, its voice was pretty deep, so, I mean, he, her, it, they could have been either.) a focused mind is the cause of happiness. A wandering mind causes unhappiness.

I told the researcher, queue, as in Netflix queue, was an interesting word. Queue is an English word. Well, not our English, England's English. Queue means line. If you had an arrangement of items in a line they would be a queueious arrangement, which by the way, is a word with the longest unbroken arrangement of vowels, seven. In English. strengths is a word with the most number of consonants with only one vowel. Eight.

I asked the interviewer, do you know the word with the most number of silent letters? Straightedge. Five. And since we say the H before the W, why isn't when spelled hwen?

What was the question?

Anyway, researchers asked if my mind was engaged in an activity with an immediate, quantifiable purpose or was it wandering? They asked me on a scale of one to ten how happy or unhappy I was.

Not really all that happy, I guess. Besides, I'm about to be replaced by a robot.

What Happened to the News?

I don't know what happened to the news. There used to be a white guy with an expensive suit and good hair whose eyes flicked to the papers he was holding and then maintained eye contact for five minutes while he told you the truth.

Women now anchor the news, too. Women have accepted a woman in the anchor chair depending on what she's wearing. Men? You know men. It depends on, well, what she's wearing.

I looked up CNN in Wikipedia, an online encyclopedia written by the retired and unemployed who make up stuff. CNN was the first all-news television network. It started out well in the beginning but there must not have been enough news, like who the next President will be and so they ran soft news. Actually, it was runny news.

Now we get minor stories about whether Hillary has brain damage, which can't compete with a major story like What Gender is Godzilla, Disney Movie Trailer the Most Irritating Ever, and Game-Changing Theme Park Rides. I don't even know what those last two mean.

See, What Gender is Godzilla isn't hard news. Besides, hard news only comes from overseas where names are hard to pronounce. You can't treat Godzilla's gender as if it were hard news because then you would have to investigate the other Godzilla genders and the courts are too busy right now trying to determine how many genders we have. After Godzillas mated you would have little Godzillas running around and I don't know about you, but I don't want to even imagine what two Godzillas mating would be like.

Granted, this is a diverting subject, as in diverting us from those boring hard news items like why you can't find work and which country we just attacked, but do I really need to know the Pentagon's plan in case of a zombie attack? And I'm not making up Pentagon Zombie Attack Plan, either.

Enter Dr. Hunter S. Thompson who invented two things - taking drugs no one had ever thought of like pineal gland extract and a new kind of journalism. Until Hunter came along, journalists tried to be fair and objective, not to be confused with Fox News' fair and objective. Thompson said badword that and mostly wrote up what his own opinions were when he wasn't shooting off firearms at random.

He invented a new genre of writing, gonzo journalism, subjectivity with extreme prejudice. You can see gonzo journalism all over the internet now in the headlines from online news magazines – Rove's Attack on Hillary Shrewd, Timothy Geithner's Unbearable Modesty, Worst Argument Ever to Ban Gay Marriage.

The writer is telling you upfront what to believe. There are embedded assumptions in all of these, like when did you quit beating your husband? What do you expect from Thompson with book titles like Fear and Loathing on The Campaign Trail?

Thompson would be laughing his head off about now if he hadn't committed suicide, been cremated, his ashes stuffed into a cannon and fired off by Johnny Depp at a drunken going away party.

Hunter made a joke but nobody got it, especially the newspapers and magazines who paid for his escapades.

So what's the joke? He wanted you to know you're on your own, kiddo. His point was, no one can be objective, even a guy in a suit with a deep voice. Especially not him. Even though I agreed with Murrow and Cronkite, no way were they objective. They had an agenda.

Thompson wanted what I want, for you to get the joke, that objective journalism is an illusion so you could see through prejudice-embedded headlines, like the ones on the internet today. I don't want the joke to be on you.

I want you to decide for yourself the truth, no matter how good his hair is or what she's wearing.

Where Your People?

"Where your people?" he had asked, hat low on his forehead, fingers jammed in his back pockets, weight leaning on one lock-kneed leg jutted out front. Something in the way I had wandered aimlessly down the street that had been my grandmother's had raised suspicion in the old man. The self-appointed neighborhood sheriff wasn't packing and I was still sober. I was likely to stay so. My people lived in a dry county.

I told him my mother had died a few years earlier. I'd come home for my father's funeral.

Where indeed where my people?

One day my son came home from school talking about what the science teacher said. See, Dad, we're not at the center of the universe. It's...

Yes, I said, we are. We are at the dead center of the universe. It didn't used to be here. It used to be at 1539 E. Woodin St. in Dallas, Texas, but it moved. Now it's here. Some day it will move again. It will be where you live. The center of the universe is wherever home is. If I've done my job, it's where you are.

Home pulses like an amoeba, starts small, grows bigger, splits, dies, or like the Phoenix, rises again.

My grandfather died before I was born. Everything happened at my grandmother's house, an impossible eleven-room wooden structure trying to collapse that accepted an endless supply of relatives down on their luck who moved in for a time, banged on it with hammers trying to nail it back together, and then moved out and on like some great plant casting its seeds on the wind.

We called my grandmother Pete. She knew my cousin Connie and I both claimed to be her favorite. She hand-sewed a C-shaped pillow she called an arm of love and tucked it around my neck. I said, I guess this puts me ahead of Connie. She said, Connie already has one.

My sister picked up the tradition after Pete died and on holidays hosted the endless supply of relatives held together by the glue of childhood. She was in the kitchen directing some second cousin I barely recognized to take out a plate of hors d'oeuvres.

She said, the best Sams has to offer. I said, you know, Pete used to make all this herself. She responded, Pete wasn't a paralegal. I don't know how much longer I can do this.

She pushed a lock of hair out of her eyes with the back of her hand, looking more like our grandmother than I would ever mention.

That fall half a continent away I stood by a stream watching a pair of salmon. I said to them, you always know where home is. I'm told you come here to mate and die. I too can hear the call that makes us turn our head toward home. When I went back to the exact spot where I began to find decay and small rooms leaning, is that what pulled me there, to accept where I came from, to hear in the wind-blown pecan the whispers of mating like you smell in the sluice and ripple of your salmon's cradle? Swimmer, show us the way to go home.

I line up my family for the ritual photo. Held in arms are babies trying to understand their brand new universe. Teens are hiding their impatience and screens behind their backs. Parents are wearing pride like new clothes, and we, grandparents with a puzzled expression, are wondering what happened? Why is everything moving at the speed of light?

My father wasn't a scientist, but he knew where the center of the Universe is.

There are ten Moore's squinting at the camera. My people are here.

It All Ends Up Here

I live at the beach. If you don't, if you're like most, you wish you did. Why is that? What is it about the edge of the earth, where the sand meets the surf?

In summer on weekends and holidays you stake your claim to your patch of sand with beer and blanket that hold your fragile family, your cute kids. Beginnings are so sweet.

But it's winter now. The rain comes in level, thin things, shingles, siding, tin signs, wind chimes, flying.

Why do you come? Is it the scent? Or for some other reason you can't quite say.

You can smell the sea before you see it, metallic, salty, some say, but it's bacteria feeding on seaweed and plankton dying. Dimethyl sulfide. Beginning and ending. The smell of birth. The smell of death.

The sea sits rocking, does it not, a deep, cold question, like the widow turning one hundred in Kansas City who said, I want to see the ocean before I die.

You're drawn here. You're drawn back.

We're closer to the truth now.

If you walk the sand some, you will see enough of death to last you a lifetime.

The beach is littered with the afterlife of broken shells your precious children bring in their hands. They spy a seagull skeleton, a feather here and there, sometimes a vortex of gulls pointing at a seal, recumbent in the rollers, its eyes picked out.

You're not the only one coming. It all ends up here, you know. When we take all the trees, clear cut the hillside, you can see in the river after a rain, the stream turn brown.

Solitary Hood, white Denali, absolute Everest, the slices of stone Himalayas, the brutal Rockies, their rough edges are being carved and smoothed. You know, of course, you can polish anything away. They will all be here one day.

Amazon, Potomac, Yellow, Blue Danube, Green River, silt carried down Big Muddy, the mighty Columbia, the river makes its bed, soiled, cleans itself. The rivers serve the sea.

You wiggle your toes in sand that was Idaho or Colorado and who can say where else?

You're using the wrong scale. Push the marks apart from decades to eons.

Give water time. We have plenty of that.

Water will have its way.

Even the earth's core will come. Volcanoes vomit boiling rock, cooled, rain-washed, worn, carried by the rivers. It will all be here some day.

You will, too. No matter where you die, Minneapolis or Mumbai, if you're kept in the Pyramids or in a vase on the mantel, given enough time, atoms equally distribute. Some particle of you, star born and still here, will come to my beach. Eventually entropy wins.

You're coming back.

You must know this now, leaning on your cane as your grandchildren bring you shells bleached to a whiteness you've understood all your life, in your bones.

I'll be here, too, to greet you, part of me, anyway.

The Meaning of Life

One of the things I value most, Daughter-in-law, is your letter asking what I thought was the meaning of life. I think you were heavily sedated at the time, but I'm still counting it.

I've spent half my life thinking about that question, half my life preparing for the end by honking my rubber chicken and half my life wondering what would happen if I filled a balloon with gasoline and tied a match...wait, that's another philosophical question.

Some tell me if we're good, at the end of life we get a fat paycheck, a big cymbal crash and stick the landing.

When my wife Joani was first diagnosed with a degenerative nerve disease she kept wondering about the future. I said, living in the future is death so we agreed we wouldn't live there. Besides, the rents are terrible. If we can do a good job just for today, then we get a tiny little cymbal crash each day.

I'm more Asian in that regard, except for kimchi. I hate kimchi. I believe in little cymbal crashes every day. That's why I help my wife, not for a big cymbal crash at the end, but for that little cymbal crash today when I make her laugh and increase the chance of getting laid.

I know you haven't seen the entire movie yet, but if you read the news you've heard how this all turns out. Some say it's not a comedy.

A wise man said there is no greater sin than having too many expectations except for voting conservative. That doesn't mean we don't plan so we won't run out of Ding Dongs. Life is what happens while we're making plans. And when I say, living in the future is death, I don't mean we have to wear dark clothes.

Sometimes when I'm repairing something, I think where's my rubber chicken? No, wait, that's not what I think. I think, what's the point since it's just going to break again? Well, for one thing, my wife told me to fix it. So I fix it and if one day it breaks again I'll hit it with a rubber chicken.

You take care of each other, not because of some big paycheck in the future, but because you love to take care of each other. You get that little cymbal crash every day. That's the meaning of life.

Or did you mean the meaning of *my* life?

Am I to believe at the end I go to a big party where I know everyone and they laugh at my jokes and it lasts for a really long time and I never get a hangover?

Or do I live my life and do all this good stuff and I just die and someone does my makeup?

Or maybe I am a crystallization of the great energy flow and when I die I'm reabsorbed and don't file taxes that year?

The point is, even if I lie in the floor and kick and scream it won't make any difference. What will make a difference? Can I make my wife laugh today?

God is a comedian. It's just hard to get him sometimes.

Gulley Jimson is dying. He starts to laugh because his paintings are hanging in the British Museum, but he doesn't have enough money to buy brushes. A nun attending him said, you'd do best to pray instead of laugh.

Jimson said, same thing, Mother.

Now, where's my rubber chicken?

About the Author

I've taught kids in middle school, college, and senior vice presidents at a Fortune 500 company, interestingly, not in that order, and no one does their homework. I have hobby-fished a dory boat launched through the surf for thirteen years from Kiwanda beach at Pacific City in Oregon. I was a paid poet. (This only means anything to other poets.) I have a novel, Pacific City, available at Amazon.

16249464R00165

Made in the USA
San Bernardino, CA
25 October 2014